Sarah Her

The Universe always delivers twice

Sarah Hertz

THE
Universe
ALWAYS
DELIVERS
twice...

MANIFESTING WITH ENERGY
AND THE LAW OF ATTRACTION

Content

CONTENT

Preface

What are miracles? A miracle according to the definition of the dictionary is an extraordinary event that contradicts the laws of nature or all experience and is therefore attributed to the direct influence of a divine power or supernatural forces, which evokes astonishment. A miracle is something which in its nature, by its degree of perfection, so far surpasses the ordinary as to evoke great admiration and great wonder.

Most people have few miracles in their lives. This book wants to change that. It wants to show you how to create more of such "miracles" in your life. But to do that, you would have to acknowledge that miracles are possible. Do you believe in miracles? What if I told you that you have a choice? Everything you believe is a choice you have made in your life consciously or unconsciously. And it's very easy to change a belief. The recipe for it is consciousness and choice. Become aware of what you believe and choose what you want to believe. I have learned and studied many spiritual and not-so-spiritual personal development and energy healing techniques over the past years. I have dug up what felt like thousands of beliefs from the depths of my subconsciousness and reprogrammed or released them using a variety of techniques. At some point I realized that all techniques work similarly because it is a choice. If you want to change something and are aware of it, you have the power. *Being conscious* is the key word here and *consciousness* is actually already the key. It is the key to making miracles.

I have loved magic since I was a kid. Magical books and fantasy in any form have accompanied me for a long time, until the outer world distracted me too much from it. But what is sober everyday life without magic and spells? Isn't it much more exciting, when you know you have the ability to create miracles in your life?

But you already know that, or you wouldn't be reading these lines. I have instructed the book to attract readers who are ready for it and who can benefit from the knowledge in this book to create miracles in their lives. Did you know that you can program things and that every "thing" has its own energy and is alive in its own way? This form of magic was practiced by our ancestors because they knew about it.[1]

I feel like *Alice in Wonderland* right now because the world is waking up and seeing that miracles are possible. More and more authors are writing books about *supernormal, metahumans, becoming supernatural,* and secret superpowers. Our universe has shifted gears and is currently accelerating our development tremendously. You may also have noticed that the last few years have been very turbulent, a pure chaos energy. Chaos creates space for something new – in your life as well as in my life and on the whole planet. Inside as well as outside. So, if it's been very turbulent in your inner or outer life lately and you've had to go through some tropical storms, it's not just you alone. The whole world is on the verge of an evolutionary leap and again the key is our consciousness.

In what felt like thousands of attempts to manifest something, I actually felt like Harry Potter at magic school. The magical world has opened its gates and it is so empowering when you suddenly awaken and realize that you don't have to continue stewing in victimhood, but can actually influence reality. Wow, are we on *Make a Wish* here? When I was a kid, I always loved watching *I Dream of Jeannie* and often wished I had a genie like that in a magic lamp. I think everyone secretly wishes that. But I started small with the wishes, first always a parking space, then amounts of money and so often flowers, because I love flowers more than anything. I've really become a flower manifestation pro. That's something that works very easily for me and it's also my first example for you of why the universe always delivers twice. Or three times. One time I had ordered flowers once again in my morning meditation and the same day I received a bouquet of tulips as a gift, a few hours later I received a big bag of bulbs to plant myself in the garden and the next day my neighbor gifted me a flower pot. I cheered to the universe for all those flowers! It works the same way for me with customers. It's not just one new order that comes in, it's always several when I order. This comes in very handy, because I can save on my marketing budget. Many beginners always rush right into their big wishes when making miracles without first building up trust in the universe and then wonder why it doesn't work out. Did you also start manifesting after *The Secret* came out and nothing happened? Or maybe something came into your life that you didn't want? Then you have surely noticed that it is not that easy. It's said that more than 94% of people who use the Law of Attraction are not successful. However, it is not that the Law of Attraction doesn't work. It works, but most people don't apply it correctly. So, what did the 6% do differently? After many years of experimenting with manifesting techniques and mountains full of books and courses on manifesting, energy healing and spiritual growth, I noticed the famous manifestation recipe was missing one important ingredient: energy! And I noticed a scheme.

That's why we will start with the magic formula for making miracles. It's very easy:

Energy x Intention = Manifestation

It doesn't matter what kind of energy you use. It can be the energy of a strong emotion or the universal energy used by techniques like *Reiki, PranaHealing, ThetaHealing* or *Reconnective Healing*. It all comes from the same energy soup. In this book, I will show you how to use the universal energy that surrounds you at all times to manifest better. By the way, I use the words universe, God, divine intelligence, quantum field, source, creation, universal consciousness interchangeably in the book. You may have your own word and belief system. For simplicity, let's agree on universe in this book so you know what is meant.

The fact that everything is energy has probably already reached you. What you may not know is that not only do you have a unique thumbprint that exists only once in this world, you also have a unique energy ID. This is something like your energetic passport, by which every other energy molecule in the universe can recognize you. You can also compare it to an IP address on a computer. So, another person always knows how to contact you telepathically.

The formula for your Energy ID[2] is as follows:

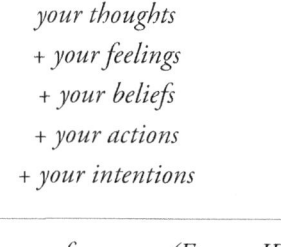

your thoughts
+ your feelings
+ your beliefs
+ your actions
+ your intentions

= your energy frequency (Energy ID)

Every thought you think, every word you speak, every feeling you have, every intention you set, everything you do and plan to do, and everything you believe in radiates its own frequency and the sum of that is you. It's therefore not static, it's constantly changing. And according to the Law of Attraction or the Law of Vibration, you attract everything into your life that vibrates on the same wavelength, so to speak. This can be the new best friend who runs into you at an event and you feel like you've known each other forever, or a tidal wave of bills because you still have a lack of awareness programmed into you about all things related to money and you've been upset with the tax office for the last three days.

In the first chapter in this book, we'll therefore look at the most important laws of the universe that you should know so that you have a solid base. And then I'll take you on a little journey into the world of energy, which I love so much and find extremely exciting.

In Chapter 2, we'll look at how you can use your energy to manifest. In Chapter 3, I'll explain how energetic blockages can sabotage your orders from the universe and how you can solve that so it works better next time. In Chapter 4, I'll show you special techniques that allow you to manifest a wish especially quickly when you're in a hurry. In Chapter 5, you'll learn to better understand the language of the universe, and in Chapter 6, why the universe doesn't know time and how you can take advantage of the knowledge of the relativity of time when manifesting. I'll show you how to use time more efficiently by stretching time or how to program a new future for yourself. All in all, I'll give you my complete knowledge that I have used to manifest big and small miracles in my life. The book concludes in the last chapter with a 21-day Miracle Challenge that gives you the opportunity to train your manifestation muscles. You can place an order with the Universe every day for these three weeks and practice manifesting with energy. I hope you have fun doing this because the Miracle Challenge will make you more aware of energies in your life.

Hopefully in this book you will learn everything it takes to make it work with big and small miracles in your everyday life. Welcome to the school for miracle makers!

So, what miracle are you wishing for currently? Write it down now and use the exercises in this book for this wish. Truly, write it down, because by writing it with your hand you already give the wish the first momentum of energy.

"Miracles arise from a mind
that is ready for them."

— A Course in Miracles

1.

Miracle Making 101 – Consciousness is the key

The human consciousness is probably the greatest riddle of our existence and we will possibly never be able to unravel this mystery completely. Quantum physics assumes that consciousness gives rise to matter. Representatives of the quantum physics are convinced that consciousness stands in interaction with the universe and the external reality is generated or at least influenced by the consciousness of the observer. That sounds pretty crazy, doesn't it?

Quantum physicists describe this phenomenon with the so-called "observer effect". It states that the material world does not exist as long as it is not perceived by a consciousness of an observer. And this is how the theory was born that the universe is a holography and that the perception of our reality is simply a projection of our consciousness. Until an observer appears, the universe is composed of a quantum field full of possibilities. And this is the crux of the matter when it comes to manifesting your wishes. You have probably already made use of the knowledge about the observer effect when you visualized your wishes or when you even already made a vision board for yourself. But there are more parameters that influence your manifestation abilities. Let's take a look at them one by one.

One for change!

"Change your vision, change your reality"

The bottom line of what quantum physicists discovered back in the 1920's is that all possibilities are always there and that the consciousness of the observer gives rise to the actual reality. So, this means that by changing your view, your reality also changes. Deepak Chopra, a world-renowned best-selling author and a pioneer in the field of mind-body healing, even postulates in his book *"Metahuman"* that we are living in a virtual reality and that the next stage in the evolution of human beings is to awaken from this illusion.[3] At the same time, not every single human being is in his or her own reality, but rather we are all in a collective virtual reality, which makes things even more complex. However, we don't want to make things unnecessarily complicated now. Just remember that your consciousness creates your reality.

How well this works with the creation of your desired reality and your manifestation, depends on which stage of development your consciousness is. The development of your consciousness takes place in different stages. Thereby your consciousness can move in different areas of your life on different stages or jump back and forth from situation to situation. So far, only 1 % of the world's population or less are enlightened in the actual sense and have reached the Buddha-consciousness (4th stage), in which everything seems to be Zen.

The 4 stages of spiritual growth and development of your consciousness:[4]

Several years ago, speaker Michael Beckwith, author and founder of the *Agape International Spiritual Center*, developed a simple model for understanding the four stages of consciousness development and spiritual growth that take us from victimhood to self-empowerment. Your life is a journey from the unconsciousness to higher consciousness.

1. **Stage – Victim consciousness:** You are convinced that things in your life just happen to you, that external circumstances determine your fate and that you are not responsible for it. You believe that you don't succeed because of your past experiences and relationships and often feel like a victim of external circumstances. Most of the time you blame others for your circumstances and troubles. Very many people remain at this stage of consciousness because they are not ready to take more personal responsibility for their lives. At this stage, the universe expresses itself "with you".

2. **Stage – Manifester consciousness:** You have made a huge development and your way of thinking has changed. You have let go of blame and are now aware that you have brought about the experiences and situations in your life. You no longer blame the circumstances in your life. You realize that you are much more powerful than you thought and consciously shape your own life. In this phase, there are many changes in your life. You begin to take control

and responsibility over your life. You learn to apply the Law of Attraction and visualize your desires. You believe that you can create your life the way you want it to be and use the power of your thoughts to do so. At this stage, you are working with the universe as a *co-creator*. The universe is now expressing itself "because of you."

3. **Stage – Channeler consciousness:** Have you ever felt that when you're doing something and you're really in the flow of it, that you just blend out everything around you? In those moments, the universe expresses itself through you. You are channeling your higher self and expressing your authenticity. In other words, who you really are. At this stage, you begin to receive a clear vision of your life. You realize which activities and which areas of life just flow and come to you completely effortlessly and without resistance, so that you even forget about time. You let yourself be guided by the universe and live your destiny. It is no longer you who is writing your story, it seems rather as if the creative force within you is expressing a story. You realize that you are part of something bigger, you give up control and no longer try to manifest something strenuously. You follow your inner voice and everything that feels easy and in the flow for you. The Universe expresses itself "through you".

4. **Stage – Being consciousness:** At the fourth stage of consciousness, you feel a deep connection to life. You become aware that you are the universe and that we are all deeply connected with one another. When you realize that your

story is not only expressed through you, but that you are, like a wave in the ocean, the living expression of this vast energetic creative force, you are awakened. You realize that your experiences serve you to experience yourself. You realize that the Universe expresses itself "as you".

Knowing these stages of development of your consciousness helps you navigate where you currently stand. This book is mainly about the second stage of consciousness and how to learn to co-create with the universe and make miracles.

Two for manifesting: Conscious and unconscious

"You create your world with your thoughts"

The wise Gautama Buddha taught: *"We are what we think, all that we are arises with our thoughts, with our thoughts we make the world."* Thoughts exist in the ethereal plane. If you want to create something – whether it is a particular job, health, or a fulfilling relationship – before all there is a thought. And thoughts are nothing other than energy.

We are often not aware of our creative power and don't even realize that we create our reality ourselves. Instead, we believe that our circumstances, other people or our own background create conditions that influence our lives. Understanding that we all manifest our experiences is not so easy, especially when we don't like our external reality. Illness, lack of money, or a theft – that's what you've manifested? Yes, you are responsible for that, too. At least the unconscious parts of you, because you manifest in two ways: consciously and unconsciously.

Unconscious manifestation comes from inner beliefs, views and convictions that we have carried for a long time. These guide our thoughts and actions in the way how we perceive our personal reality. Collective beliefs, that is, thought patterns that we have absorbed through our social environment and society, also influence us. So does the information from our ancestors that we have inherited and that is stored in our cells.

When you become aware that you are the consciousness that creates your life and you realize which beliefs you identify with – that is, when you can observe your ego, thoughts and emotions – you can change them, too! Here and now, in this moment, you can step into your creative power and hold the magic wand with which you can consciously create your life and manifest into your life the experiences you want to have. You can thus give your life a completely different depth and quality. The potential of your consciousness will possibly be the greatest discovery of your life. And yet, you will probably never be able to fully grasp it, because your true potential exceeds your current imagination by far.

Three for limitless: experiencing, having and being

"There are no limits to what you can experience, have and be"

To grasp the consciousness with the mind is not exactly easy, because it is limitless and not localizable. You can expand it in all directions, into infinity, it will never stop anywhere. In the same way the possibilities of your consciousness are endless. You can experience, have and be anything. The only limits your consciousness can experience are the ones you set for it. The universal consciousness is just waiting to be discovered by you. In everyday life, consciousness is not necessarily a state that we can describe so accurately. We are talking more about mindfulness and being aware of a moment in which you manage to be present in the here and now. Or a moment in which you are in the position of the observer and observe yourself, for example, right now as you are reading these lines and at the same time are hungry. You observe yourself from the seat of your higher self, but no human being knows where that actually is. The human mind cannot be measured or detected in our central nervous system. All our perceptions, sensations, memories and ideas are part of this intangible consciousness, which for the shamans since ancient times is the miraculous energy that connects us with everything and is the reason for our existence. It is possible for our consciousness to reinvent itself at any time and to free itself from all self-imposed limitations. In order for you to experience the boundlessness of your consciousness, we will now do an exercise.

Exercise: Expansion Meditation

Close your eyes and become aware of your body. Feel the limits of your body, where do you end and where does the couch begin, which you are sitting on? Feel how your breath automatically flows in and out. Sense how you feel. Now feel yourself in all directions, sense your aura and your energy field. Now imagine how it expands, first five meters in all directions. Up, down, left, right, forward and backward. Now you expand your energy field 500 meters in all directions, then 1,000 kilometers. Then

10,000 kilometers. Feel with each breath how your consciousness expands until it encompasses the whole earth, and on and
on. You are now as big as the galaxy, and with each breath you
are becoming lighter and bigger. You are now infinite consciousness and one with the divine life force. If you wish, stay in this
state for a few minutes and fill up with energy. You are always
connected with everything; limits only exist in your mind.

Four for vibration: Atoms, neutrons, protons & energy

"Everything is energy"

Experiments by quantum physicists have shown that what
we call matter is 99.99999 % nothing. In his famous formula
$E=mc^2$, Einstein has already shown that mass and energy can
be converted into each other. Mass is simply compressed energy
and no longer so invisible. But it still consists of the same frequencies and vibrations or energy waves.

Our whole universe consists of energy. There is nothing
which does not consist of energy. Everything in our universe
is made up of the same elementary particles that the Big Bang
created. If you're a fan of the TV show *Big Bang Theory*, be aware
that it is actually not a theory any more, but that gravitational
waves of the Big Bang have already been detected. Atoms are like
the smallest Lego parts in our world. And these in turn consist
of protons, neutrons and electrons. Strictly speaking, an atom
consists of only about 0.00000001 % matter, everything else
is energy. Lynne McTaggert, in her book *"The Field"*, has em-
barked on an exciting search for the primordial cosmic energy

and has shown that science is now following spiritual teachings and proving that we are moving in an intelligent energy field (zero-point field) that permeates everything and everyone.[5] Some call it God, others quantum field or universe. Dr. Joe Dispenza says you can think of the quantum field as a single, vast, invisible database whose information you can access through your central nervous system.[6] When you align your consciousness with that of the quantum field – that is, become pure consciousness – you have access to all possibilities that exist as potential and can bring them into existence with your consciousness.

"If you want to find the secrets of the Universe,
think in terms of energy, frequency and vibration."

— Nikola Tesla, physicist

1.1

You are the Universe, or as Obi Wan said: "May the Force be with you"

We are in for a paradigm shift as significant as when most people thought the Earth was a flat disc. So, we have learned that the universe was created by the Big Bang, a huge cosmic explosion. But what came before that? Mankind has been racking its brains over this question for millennia. I don't have an answer either, but there are cosmologists, such as Deepak Chopra and physicist Menas Kafatos, who have made the effort to find a new answer based on the latest parallel findings of physics and spirituality in their book *"You Are the Universe"*.[7] When I first heard about the universe being conscious and alive and always evolving just like us, I almost fell off my chair. No joke, I found it *mind-blowing* and somehow it made total sense. Is the universe therefore alive and able to respond to us humans? According to Chopra and Kafatos, science points to just that. The universe responds to what we think and what we do. It is practically a *human* universe. But there is also no universe without our interaction and someone perceiving it. The latest research in physics supports this new worldview. Light is both particle and wave, and changes behavior when observed. You remember the observer effect? The authors postulate, *"the greatest mystery is not that the universe is alive and conscious, but that humans create their own reality – and then forget what they have done."*[7] Each human is a *co-creator* of the cosmic reality. Actually, this worldview is not all that new. As early as ancient India, Vedic scriptures speak of *Aham Brahmasmi*, which translates as *"I am the universe"* or *"I am all that is."* [8]

Therefore, you are not an inhabitant of a planet just racing through space without a plan, but you are a creative co-creator of our collective reality. Hallelujah! It is about time that we use the creative powers of our mind better in the future than for complaining like e.g., Michael, who always sits unhappy at his desk or co-worker Susi, who gossips about her neighbors every day.

As humans, we are complex energy fields with a consciousness within the overall consciousness of the universe. The omnipresent quantum field holds unlimited possibilities, experiences and information, from which you can draw, for you are a *metahuman*, as Deepak Chopra puts it. You are not limited to the experiences you have as a human, but are an infinite being with superpowers. Yes, that's right, real supernatural superpowers. Haven't you always secretly wanted to have superpowers like *Superman*, *Wonder Woman* or *The Flash*? These superpowers give you the opportunity to live in a universe beyond your imagination and even more fascinating than all your dreams. By the way, your intuition is one of your special superpowers! You can freely shape your reality according to your wishes with these powers, as some monks do, who live in the mountains and make water boil or move things with the power of their thoughts alone. If it is not a pot of boiling water with which you could cook your noodles for dinner, you can use your superpowers to manifest whatever you want. It works faster and does not need 40 years of meditation training.

Your superpowers may still be hidden, otherwise you probably wouldn't be reading this book. The reason why you are not yet a professional in manifesting is also hidden: in your subconsciousness. Your creative power is guided by your consciousness, which in turn is influenced by your subconsciousness, your beliefs and habits. These are formed by your experiences and your social environment and are often linked to negative thinking. Over many years we unconsciously program our thinking around limiting beliefs such as *"I can't do this"*, *"I'm not good enough"* or even *"no one loves me"*, which trigger negative emotions in us and steer our manifestations in the wrong direction. An emotion is nothing more than energy in motion (E-motion). Negative thoughts and emotions rob you of your creative energy and don't allow you to realize what special powers are within you. Don't worry, this is not your fault. Our brain is still in survival mode from Neanderthal times and lags a bit behind the new worldview in development. It is simply important that you now become aware of the thoughts that are floating around in your head during the day and not let them run on autopilot. (You'll learn how to solve this problem in Chapter 3). The universe responds to your subconscious beliefs that float beneath the surface and often go unrecognized. Again and again, it sends you situations and experiences which vibrate on the frequency of your convictions and again only confirm to you what you believe in deep inside. Why this is so, I will explain to you in the following chapter with the laws which work in the universe. Did you know that gravity is nothing more than curved space-time? And that time is relative, you have surely already heard, right? The clocks go slower on earth than in space. Einstein has already proved mathematically that time, space, matter and energy are interchangeable. But there are still further laws in the universe which have influence on your manifestation power. Just remember at this point: *Your outer reality is a reflection of your inner beliefs.* And that is why it is so important that your inner beliefs match the reality you want to live.

You fortunately have the free choice to change your beliefs and your inner world – and therefore your outer world. If you want to manifest successfully, you have no choice but to get rid of your limiting beliefs that have snuck into your subconscious mind and became firmly anchored there. But don't worry, you have the power within you to dissolve your limitations at the speed of light. May the Force be with you, as Obi Wan Kenobi so aptly said in *Stars Wars*.

1.2

The 12 Laws of the Universe

There is a certain order in the universe, even if it may appear like a huge chaos to the naked eye. There is order, because laws operate in the universe. Laws of nature exist, like the law of gravity or the law of the speed of light. These laws don't apply however for example to our thoughts. Cosmic laws also exist. For instance, in the book *"Kybalion"* the most important seven hermetic laws have been written down, laws, which are said to have been channeled by Hermes, the Greek god of wisdom.[10] Based on this, the 12 universal laws have been described, which can help you to understand the connections.

Without an awareness of these cosmic laws, it can happen that you feel lost at times or think that you are hitting a brick wall or that the Law of Attraction just doesn't work for you. If you realize that there are more forces at play, it will be easier for you to pay attention to them, just as you take gravity seriously in your life and preferably don't drop anything that can break.

If you want to manifest successfully together with the universe, you should know the following 12 laws:[11]

1. **The Law of Vibration**
   Everything in the universe vibrates on energy waves, also called frequencies, just like radio waves. For example, if you look at water molecules under a microscope, you will see

that they vibrate. And everything that vibrates also emits a frequency. And that in turn is energy, which means that everything in the universe is energy. You too are energy, as are your thoughts and your emotions and everything else in your life. You have a unique energy frequency (Energy ID) that is constantly changing. As you change your frequency, you also change the experiences you have in your life.

2. The Law of Attraction

This law of the universe is probably the best known and has many similarities with the law of vibration. However, it is subordinate to it. It says that the same attracts the same. Hence, in order to attract what you wish into your life, you must match your frequency to the frequency of your fulfilled wish. This works partly by seeing your wish as already fulfilled and being grateful for it, but overall, your Energy ID must vibrate at the same frequency as your wish. Generally, this means that if you are positive, kind and grateful, you will attract more such things into your life. If you are predominantly angry, pessimistic or depressed, you attract more of these vibrations into your life.

3. The Law of Inspired Action

This law is often forgotten when it comes to manifesting. Your desire will not come true if you simply visualize professional success, health or a fulfilling love relationship and continue to sit on the couch. You must become active and take action to experience change in your material world.

4. The Law of Divine Oneness

Everything in the universe is interconnected. We are all one with the universe. Everything you do has an effect on the collective consciousness and the universe. There is no separateness between anyone and anything. We humans are all connected as well. This is the reason telepathy works so well between some people, or why a mother can feel when something happens to her child 1.000 kilometers away.

5. The Law of Correspondence

This law states that your outer reality is a reflection of your inner world. As within so without, as above so below – this is also described by the hermetic laws in the *Kybalion*. You have certain experiences in your life because you hold certain beliefs. If you want changes in your life, you have to start with changes in yourself.

6. The Law of Cause and Effect

This law is also known as the law of karma. All your actions have an effect. If you direct your actions toward the good of your fellow man, the universe will do good to you as well. Give and take is a cycle that should always be in balance. By recognizing that the causes of your experiences are your own past actions, you can learn to accept both your good and your bad experiences, and to direct your actions in such a way that leads to more harmony.

7. The Law of Compensation

An important law if you want to manifest money. In order to receive money, you must first add value. You must give before you can take. Be interested, not interesting. Ask questions, pay attention to others, listen and help if you can with your abilities. If you help other people fulfill their wishes, yours will be fulfilled. So, if you want more money, help others make more money. If you want to be happy, make other people happy.

8.   The Law of Perpetual Transmutation of Energy

This law states that everything is in a constant state of change. The energy of the universe is always moving and transforming into physical form and out again. Like the particles that are perpetually changing from wave to particle. On the one hand, the law points to the fact that everything shows up in physical form at some point, so your thoughts become things. On the other hand, that high vibrations (happiness, love, joy) can transform and influence low vibrations (sadness, shame). But it is also the law by which you can see that everything has to change all the time. There is no standing still in your life, everything must be in a constant state of flux.

9.   The Law of Relativity

Everything is neutral. There is no good or bad energy. Emotions, actions or experiences are evaluated as something good or bad only when we compare them to something else. Challenges are also relative and dependent on your perspective. Things are not as bad as they may seem at first glance. The events in your life are not working against you, they are happening for you. It is only a question of perspective. In every challenge there is opportunity to learn and grow.

10. The Law of Polarity

You wanted to manifest something, but instead of your wish coming true, something completely opposite has entered your life that you didn't want at all? Don't worry, it can happen. And actually, that's a good thing, because polarity creates clarity: you get what you don't want, so you get a clear vision of what you do want. And once you know exactly what you want, you'll move in the right direction with a lot more power.

Sometimes when you go through something difficult, something wonderful comes out of it into your life.

11. The Law of Rhythm

Everything runs in cycles. Just as the seasons appear in cycles, life also has its own rhythm. You can't always harvest fruit, there are phases, when you must sow seeds and patiently watch the sprouts grow. And sometimes old leaves have to fall off so that something new can blossom again. Inspiration, creativity and activity have their own cycle and are not always there, but come back as surely as the next summer.

12. The Law of Gender

There are two types of energy: female and male. Male energy is active and female energy is receptive. Both belong to the whole. They might be opposites, but they are nevertheless two facets of the same force and form a unity. In order for harmony to prevail, both energies must combine and a balance must be created between the two. In life, we are drawn to the opposite pole again and again, quite automatically, in order to be able to have this experience and transform it into a holistic experience. We are confronted with people and circumstances that express the opposite of ourselves so that we can experience what we are not. Through these experiences you get the opportunity to discover what elements are missing in your life, what qualities you want to develop to remove the polarity and be complete.

All these 12 cosmic laws can have an effect on all aspects of your life and play a role in manifesting. Not everything in life always goes as planned. Sometimes things take an unexpected course, but often things are not as they appear to you at first glance. If you change your perspective and think about which law might be at work here, they can suddenly have a completely different meaning. Don't delay, ask the universe today :-). Remember, you have now learned that you are a team in manifesting and that you can talk to each other.

"We're never separate from the quantum field.
Most people are just unaware of it
and if you're unaware of it,
it doesn't exist for you."

– Dr. Joe Dispenza

1.3

A miracle rarely comes alone

You certainly know the saying "What goes around comes around". This explains the Law of Vibration in one sentence. It works always and everywhere, in every moment and if you take it seriously down to your smallest cell, you have the key in your hand to influence and change cause and effect. In short, your entire reality. I didn't say it was easy, though. It requires a lot of consciousness, choice and your will.

For you to be on the same wavelength with the universe when placing your orders, so to speak, it is important to re-member that everything is energy and everything vibrates. The Universe always responds to you in form of vibrations and fre-quencies. Gabby Bernstein teaches that the number one key to making miracles is to cultivate the energy of what you want to experience and witness.[12] What does the energy of your miracle feel like?

Let's take the flower example. When I order flowers, I feel the energy of flowers, I feel the beauty in my mind, I smell the wonderful scent, I take pleasure in the delicacy, grace, and beau-tiful colors of the blossoms. I immerse myself in the energy of flowers. Or let's say you want to manifest money. This will not work if you have limiting beliefs that say *"money sucks"* or *"if you want money, you are greedy"*. This is not the energy of money that you desire. That energy would probably trigger a flood of bills instead. So, if you want to manifest money, immerse yourself in the energy of what money enables you to do and how happy you are about it. It's usually never about money, but about what it stands for. What is your actual desire that you want to make possible with the money? Why don't you order that right away, but take the detour via money? The universe will always provide you with people, experiences and miracles that correspond to your vibrational frequency. You can say the affirmation *"I am rich"* a thousand times, but if you don't feel rich, you will not attract wealth.

Have you ever had a streak of bad luck and one misfortune after another happens? That is simply the echo of the energies you are emitting, whether consciously or unconsciously. This does not mean that you should suppress your feelings in the future, quite the opposite. Don't suppress them and don't go into resistance, then, for example, anger and resentment can flow through you instead of getting stuck in your energy field and attracting more anger or resentment in the future as an energetic blockage. You'll learn more about energetic blockages in chapter 3.

By the way, the universe doesn't deliver just once. A sound also doesn't come back just once, but in the form of an echo, always several times. I experienced a funny example with socks. One morning while getting dressed I thought to myself *"I need new socks"*. Apparently, however, there was a firm intention behind it, because I meant it seriously, I really needed new socks again. No kidding, when I went out the door an hour later, there was a pair of my socks on the patio table, freshly washed. When I went to the beach in the afternoon, I also found a pair of colorful socks on a bench there, apparently someone forgot them there. On the way back, I stopped at my neighbor's house, who had just returned from a trip. There was a suitcase open in the hallway of his house, packed to the top with green socks. I literally laughed out loud, that was too funny dear universe, you mean well :-). The socks were giveaways from his company to hand out at an exhibition. And well, guess what, of course he also gave me some socks without me telling him about my unconscious order in the morning. Oh yeah, and the next day friends came back from a ski trip and gifted me some cozy ski socks. I celebrated the universe, such a great delivery service! Something similar happened to me with cucumbers when I innocently thought *"I need a cucumber"* while cooking. The next day there was a cucumber on the patio table – no joke! I have a neighbor with a huge garden who grows vegetables, he probably put it there as a gift – you see the universe mostly works through other people. As you can see, you are actually manifesting all the time, whether you sit down and order consciously or just order casually, the universe is listening the whole time. Big Brother is watching you :-).

It also works with specific orders. I can define exactly what I want and attract the energy from that desire (with the exercise you will learn in chapter 2). For example, I once ordered customers who would buy several of my products at once, i.e., order large quantities, which is not usually the case. Within 2 days I had requests from 5 customers, all of whom wanted 10–20 orders of my products. A friend of mine, who used this technique wanted to be on the cover of a women's magazine. She used the technique from chapter 2 and then appeared almost simultaneously on two covers of women's magazines shortly after she had placed the wish.

I'm not going to tell you any fairy tales, with some things it works quickly and easily for me and with other things not so much yet, such as on the love front. It works wonderfully with date orders or dinner invitations, but the soul mate is still missing, lol :-). However, I know that in these cases other forces are at work and I need to work on myself or just be patient a bit longer. You will learn what can sabotage your orders or why it does not yet work smoothly for all things in chapter 3.

Before that, however, we will take a look at how exactly the magic formula for making miracles is composed. I will now show you how you can manifest with energy and what is important when ordering. But what I can give you 100 % is that the Universe always delivers twice – or three times or many times more.

"The Universe always has your back."

– Gabrielle Bernstein

2.

The Magic Formula for Making Miracles – Manifesting with Energy

Let's now go into depth about how exactly miracle making works. I have already told you my magic formula, but it's still very helpful to become more *conscious* of what exactly is important when manifesting. I emphasize the word *conscious*, because it is not a question of whether you manifest, but whether you do it consciously. Consciousness is the key to wonderland. You are not an unrealistic dreamer if you believe in miracles. On the contrary, only by opening and expanding your consciousness, you can break the limits of the standard world order, which is still based on fear and scarcity. To create miracles that help earth and humanity with the next evolutionary leap, you have to become more aware so that the supernatural can make its way into normality. And it's already doing that right now, with more and more people believing in magic again. In the book *"Real Magic: Ancient Wisdom, Modern Science, and a Guide to the Secret Power of the Universe"*, Dean Radin scientifically clarifies how supernatural phenomena work that used to be declared witchcraft and magic.[13] And he shows how everything is directly related to our consciousness. You are only capable of experiencing what your consciousness can grasp. Actually, all new experiences are miracles because you may simply not have thought of them as being possible before. You know the famous saying *"I'll believe it when I see it!"*? In reality, you'll see it when you believe it.

"Be wise and stick to miracles."

— Masha Kaleko

2.1

The Genie in the Magic Lamp
is your brain

You don't need a genie in the magic lamp to grant you your wishes. You are the genie yourself. Let me explain why.

Albert Einstein and Thomas Edison have scientifically proven that the brain continuously emits energies and frequencies that can be measured. These frequencies vibrate higher than radio frequencies. Scientists today still have difficulty understanding how radio waves can be received by satellites and that frequencies can be everywhere and pass through all matter. Just because you can't see them with the naked eye doesn't mean they don't exist. Everything on our Earth is made of atoms, which are made of neutrons and electrons, which in turn are made of energy. Everything consists of the same material in our universe, only the combination of atoms and frequencies differs. And the number of potential frequencies is infinite.

However, for the sake of not making it too complicated, all you need to know at this point is that your brain can emit and receive energies. It works sort of like the antenna of a radio tower or radio. These frequencies affect physical matter and all matter is made up of energies that vibrate differently. Everything on this planet and every cell of your body emits a frequency. The frequencies from your brain, that is, your thoughts, are the most powerful because they travel faster than the speed of light. They are instantaneous and even bypass space and time.

Your mind has the creative ability to create thoughts in two ways. First, you can *think* a thought, which is the voice in your head that you hear. Second, you can imagine (visualize) a picture, which is also a thought. So, whether you say *"blue elephant"* or visualize it, it is both a thought. Everything arises from an initial thought. Einstein sat in his armchair for endless hours doing thought experiments before proving them with mathematics. It all originated in his imagination first. This is the miracle machine in your brain that has the ability to think creatively and come up with something that can even enable humanity to go to Mars. No other species can do that, all others still behave the same way as they did a thousand years ago. Humans evolve through the wonderful gift of their creative minds, the genie in their brains … The question is, what do you do with this wonderful brilliant mind? Do you use it in creative ways to manifest your desires or do you spend hours getting upset with your co-worker whose work you had to do today?

However, there are also thoughts that your brain, or rather you, don't create yourself, but that your mind thinks on auto-pilot. This voice in your head is like a monkey gone wild, never stopping to chatter, sometimes thinking the stupidest thoughts that are not helpful to you at all, and on top of that, all that chatter makes up 95% of your total thoughts. Why does your mind do that and why are most of them so negative? We'll go into this in more detail in Chapter 3.4.

So, if we now assume that our thoughts determine our reality, we'd be in quite a mess, wouldn't we? Let's remember, the Law of Attraction states that there is a magnetic attraction between similar frequencies, and the stronger the magnetic match, the stronger the attraction. This means that the frequencies you send out with your brain attract the exact same ones. Your circumstances, your current and future external reality, match your frequencies at every moment. All kinds of experiences, situations, things, feelings and thoughts that match the frequencies you are sending out will come into your life. The universe can become quite eager and deliver you for example several unordered bills, if you are angry about the same thing for several days and cannot let it go in your mind. For example, a friend had wished for peace and quiet and more time for herself. Promptly there were interlocking problems and the train she was on was at an indefinite standstill. They had to wait almost two hours for it to continue and so she had plenty of time and rest instead of already being hectic at work. That same evening, her friends canceled dinner, so she could look forward to a cozy evening at home. Suddenly, time and rest were there in abundance. The frequency between what you think and what comes into your life is always the same. Therefore, to manifest your wish, you must match the frequency of your thoughts to the frequency of what you desire. It's like adjusting a station on the radio. You turn your own frequency to attract the frequency of your fulfilled wish – and you do this with the power of your thoughts and your will. Louise Hay is probably the most famous example. She has inspired millions of people to change their lives by changing their thoughts.[14] Your thoughts are like a GPS by which your life unfolds.

"Your thoughts create your tomorrows."

— Louise Hay

2.2

Intention is your magic wand

If you want to create miracles, you need a magic wand like Harry Potter – you might think. But did you know, that your intention works like an invisible wand? Thoughts can actually influence reality when they are laser focused. An intention is the plan to perform a certain action, it's like a laser beam of focused energy. So, an intention is a focused thought that has much more energy than a normal thought. Lynne McTaggert has researched numerous experiments in her book *"The Intention Experiment"* that prove how much intention can influence reality.[15] She herself also starred in the famous spiritual cult film *"What the bleep do we know?"*. She shows, for example, how you can make plants grow 10% faster with your intention or change the structure of water and thus clean up polluted water. The whole thing goes so far that many people with the same intention can even influence global warming or violence in certain regions.

Your intentions thus have a huge impact on the experiences you have in your life. You always get what you focus on. And your focus is determined by your intention. Energy always follows attention. If you learn how to place your focus on what you want to manifest by setting intentions, it will be much easier for you to attract wonderful experiences into your life. What you focus on grows because it gets more energy. When you set intentions, you put your focus on what you want to experience.

By doing this, you increase the likelihood of those things happening.

It is very important that you understand the difference between a wish and an intention: A wish is closely connected with emotions, specifically with *"I want this"* and *"I don't have this"*-emotions. An intention, on the other hand, has much more of a clear aim. You align your will with your intention. *"Thy will be done"* is not just a saying in the Bible. With an intention you declare to the universe that you will create something or make something happen. There is a belief behind it that it is possible. Intentions are really a great tool when you want to make your dreams come true, but they are not a wish list.

In order to make miracles you therefore need clear intentions and the belief that they are possible. Imagine that you want to get a croissant at the bakery for breakfast. You know you have change in your pocket and you can run over to the bakery and get the croissant. You don't doubt that you can actually accomplish this intention, but are absolutely certain that you will enjoy a croissant for breakfast. Set your intention with the same feeling of certainty. Now, before you go off and frantically wave your invisible magic wand, let me show you what else is important. Lynne McTaggert recommends the following process when setting intentions:[16]

1. Everything is a choice. What change do you want to make? What do you want to manifest? Do you know this feeling?: You're scrolling through Instagram again and you think to yourself, I want to have a life that great. And suddenly a negative feeling is building up inside you because you

haven't experienced anything exciting this week. A great tool to avoid falling into such a thought trap are intentions. Choose a thought that will always have your back. Start small, e.g., with a thought for today or tomorrow.

2. Before you set your intention, put your body in a calm position. Take a few deep breaths or meditate for a few minutes. It also helps to always set the intention in the same place, as this will charge the place with your positive thoughts.

3. Define your specific intention. You can use your feelings to help you with this, how do you want to feel? In the Instagram example, an intention like *"I am brave and explore the world"* or *"I experience something beautiful every day"* could help you.

4. Now you need to energize your intention. Make use of the Law of Vibration and raise your frequency. Feel how the outcome would feel. Feel the excitement of anticipation of the outcome. Bring your attention to your heart or breathe through it a few times to increase your heart magnetic field. Feeling compassion or gratitude is also enough to charge the intention. Living in the energy and being the energy of your intention in everyday life helps to manifest this intention.

5. You can think of an intention as a balloon. When you have filled it with energy, let it fly. Intentions are like floating thought forms that develop a life of their own. Famous magicians, by the way, used to create so-called elementals

with the magical ingredients of "strong will," "clarity," and "conscious intentions" – thought forms that have an intelligence of their own.[17] Thought forms are creations of ethereal energy. The difference with an intention is simply the control and amount of energy used.

Setting an intention is like planting seeds in the ground. You trust that something wonderful will grow from it.

I like to start my day with an intention. When I set an intention in my morning meditation to go through my day energized and having fun with the things I'm going to do that day, I always have great experiences throughout my day. Jose Silva calls this principle **"segmenting"** – you divide your day into many small segments and set an intention for each segment in your morning meditation, or visualize in this way how you want your day to unfold.[18]

The universe then provides me with all sorts of things that match the frequency of that intention. The other day, a friend who owns a coffee shop dropped off some homemade energy balls made from dates and nuts, completely unexpectedly. She had tried a new recipe for her guests and wanted my opinion. That made my morning so much more fun for me! Why don't you try it out, you can't lose anything and maybe you'll attract some yummy snacks, too! And since so many things coincide with the frequency of *"going through the day full of energy and having fun"*, the universe has all sorts of ways to deliver the order. And it's very happy to do so several times.

On this day I actually felt so good that I decided to go jogging on the beach, which otherwise happens very rarely, as I am rather lazy when it comes to sports. I also had time for a midday nap, which gave me more energy for the afternoon. My meeting in the afternoon then was very fun, as I enjoyed the creative teamwork so much. You'll find out for yourself that your intention in the morning will have a direct impact on the experiences you have throughout your day.

Your car, by the way, also provides you with a great opportunity to set intentions for yourself on a regular basis: Every time you sit down in your car, you can take the opportunity to set an intention for yourself. For example, *"I will get to my destination quickly and safely"*. The idea behind this is as follows: The more often you set yourself a certain intention, the faster these thoughts will become your routine and after a few repetitions you will automatically get into your car with the intention that you have now set yourself several times. From now on you will always arrive quickly and safely at your destination. By regularly setting a certain intention, you reprogram your brain and turn your intentions into a natural thought process. Other places can also serve as **anchors** for you. For example, every time you enter your kitchen, you can set the intention *"I give my body what it needs"*, promoting healthy eating.

What miracle do you want to manifest now? Let's take as an example that you want to start your own business. With an appropriate intention, you communicate to the universe what you want to create. The Universe will help you by providing all sorts of things that resonate with the frequency of your miracle and intention. It will send the right people into your life at the right time, it will give you experiences that will steer you in the right direction, or it will send you the ideas that will enable you to land your first clients. When synchronicities like this happen to you, you know it's a positive feedback loop to your intention. You already see an echo coming back to you and so you know that your desire is about to manifest.

The likelihood of you manifesting the red Tesla at the beginning of your manifestation career may not be that high, unless your belief is on board from the beginning. I actually know someone who ordered a Tesla and manifested the missing amount using the exercise in Chapter 2.3. He wanted a very specific piece of equipment, but lacked the money for it. Due to some synchronicities, there were misunderstandings and a delivery bottleneck that resulted in him getting the equipment he wanted for free along with it as compensation.

If you have manifested a small or bigger miracle for the first time, it will strengthen your faith in the universe many times over and motivate you to continue. Manifesting is something you have to practice, practice and practice. The stronger your faith in the Universe becomes, the easier and faster you will be able to manifest more miracles. And most importantly, don't think about how the universe will manifest your wish. That would only create doubt in you. Right now, you don't know the ways and means needed to realize your wish. And that is not important. The universe takes care of the *How*. All it wants is your trust. Your trust in the universe and its laws. They work. Always. Now let's do an exercise to strengthen your faith that your orders will truly always be delivered.

Exercise:
How to Build Faith in the Universe as Strong as an Ox[19]

For this exercise, you'll need a piece of paper and a pen. Write down what you would like to manifest within the next six months. Successful people know their goals and what direction they are going in. Most importantly, successful people write down their goals. Truly, it's important that you write with a pen and not with a keyboard. This is where the magic seems to lie! By writing down your wishes with your hand, you can actually feel your thoughts, giving them an extra boost of energy.

1. **Write a list of all the things you desire.** What do you want to experience? Who would you like to be? What do you want to have? You may think that only a few of these wishes will actually come true. Write on this list really all your wishes, if money would not be a factor, if there would be no limitations or reservations and nobody would tell you that your wishes are unrealistic and you would know that the wish will come true. What could that be? It could be material things or non-material things (maybe you want to be able to play a new instrument).

2. **Rate your belief on a scale of 10 to 1.** Go through all your wishes and write next to each wish how much you believe it will come true within the next six months. 10 stands for you have absolute faith that your wish will come true, 1 stands for you have absolutely no faith at all. It is important that you don't think long about how much faith you have in the

fulfillment of a wish, but intuitively write down the first number that comes into your head.

3. **With this list you can now start manifesting.** You will manifest all the wishes you have written down. However, it is important that you start with the goals and dreams that you believe you can manifest. Focus first on the wishes that you have rated a 10.

Which of your wishes create great anticipation in you and awaken a tingling inside you just thinking about them coming true? First, pick the wishes that make you feel incredibly good, that you feel a burning desire for. Wishes that get you into the *sweet spot*, where the frequencies of your thoughts have extra power to attract equal frequencies because of those great feelings. It should always be your goal to get into the *sweet spot*, because this is where your manifestation power is boosted many times. Which wishes do you think will come true with ease (wishes with ratings 8–10)? When you manifest these wishes and experience that ordering from the universe really works out, even though you may have had no idea at the beginning how your wish should come true, your faith will strengthen. And your faith in the universe, in yourself and your creative power, is the key.

"You get in your life what you think
about most of the time."

– Earl Nightingale

2.3

Energy fuels your wishes

Much of what is taught about manifesting teaches us to invest in our minds and use our thoughts as tools. However, this is only half the truth. Your thoughts do send the electrical signals to the universe, but how does the universe send the appropriate frequencies back to you? Neuroscientist Dr. Joe Dispenza teaches us that heightened emotions create a magnetic field in your heart that draws the frequencies back to you, much like a magnet in fact. However, if you assume that you are pulling the frequencies out of the future back to you, it won't work. The trick is, and this is why all gurus actually say this, to experience your future in the here and now as if it has already happened. Experience the feelings in your heart as if your desire has already manifested. Be the energy you want to experience. You dive into the quantum field, tune into the frequency that is already there as one of infinite possibilities, choose it and attract it energetically-magnetically. Dr. Joe has researched in over 7,000 brain scans how a coherent brain sends out the signal and a coherent heart draws the feeling and desired event back to you. When you open your heart and feel a higher emotion, such as gratitude or love, heart coherence and a magnetic field the size of a car is created. The energy you generate, in that case, is the fuel for your wish, it carries the information out into the universe at the speed of light, and your heart magnetic field pulls it back to you.[20] So that's one possible scientific explanation according to Dr. Joe. A number of people have experienced miracles and spontaneous healings on and after his seven-day retreats, so much so that they now sell out in minutes.

In various energy healing techniques, which I have learned over the years, energy also has been used to charge the intention. In *Prana Healing*, for example, universal life energy is first channeled and radiated onto the earth, and when the energy is flowing really strongly at the end of the meditation, it is also used for one's own intentions. First give, then take. In *Theta Healing*, it works similarly, where you go to the 7th level of existence in meditation, which is the quantum field or the divine source and give your intention there. *Reiki* and *Reconnective Healing* are healing frequencies of universal energy that mainly dissolve your energetic blockages so that your energy can flow freely again. Goals and visions can also be manifested with it. So, you can use your own energy or channel the universal life energy to give your wish the energy it needs.

There is another technique that I learned from *Access Consciousness*. This one has become my very favorite because it works so well and because it gives you limitless energy. *Energy pulls* are truly a magical tool when it comes to creating a new reality for yourself.[21] Pulling energy takes a bit of practice. It's not something you do with your mind. Rather, you're tapping into a primal wisdom of your body. It knows how to do it; you can't really go wrong. Do you realize that you are in an infinite ocean of energy? The universe is full of energy. The energy is flowing through you every second, through your central meridian, through your chakras, it is flowing continuously. The energy is all around you, you can even pull energy molecules from your surroundings to you when you are tired and recharge yourself with new life energy. You've probably heard that you can hug a tree to ground and recharge yourself with energy. Well, it works similar to that, you just don't need to take the detour via the tree anymore.

Let's try it out right now. By the way, this exercise is the cornerstone for the Miracle Challenge at the end of the book. *Energy pulls* need to be practiced – it's like playing an instrument, you have to practice before you can play a song and that's why I invite you to practice it. The more and the longer you pull energy from the universe, the more fuel your wish has.

Exercise: Energy Pulls – Charge your wish with energy

First think about what you want to manifest.

1. Contact the universe by doing the expansion meditation from page 21. You are now infinitely large and connected to the universe.

2. Send your order with an intention or a question (see chapter 2.4), e.g. *"Dear Universe, why am I having such a great adventure journey?"* or *"Dear Universe, thank you that I am having such a great adventure journey"*.

3. Now feel the energy of it. How would it feel if you had a magic wand and the wish had already come true? Form a ball of energy with your hands in front of your solar plexus

chakra. Take the energy and fill the energy ball in your mind with the energy you feel when, for example, you experience a great adventure. This could be pure happiness, joy and excitement. Put into the energy ball everything else you wish for.

4. Now pull energy from the entire universe into this energy ball. You don't need to know exactly how this works. Just imagine in your mind how you attract energy from all directions – from above and below, behind you and in front of you. If you are sensitive, you can even feel the ball of energy in your hands expanding, filling with energy and getting bigger and bigger until you are sitting in a big ball of energy yourself. Feels good, doesn't it? Keep pulling and pulling and pulling. Do this quietly for a few minutes. When it gets warm in your heart, your heart is just opening up thanks to all the energy you are pulling into your energy ball and through you.

5. When you feel a tingling all over, send small beams of energy back into the universe to all the people, events and synchronicities that will help you bring your wish to fruition. Thank the Universe that your wish will come true with ease and as quickly as possible.

6. That's it, let go of everything. Don't think about how your wish will manifest. You don't have to know, and you don't have to make any effort for your wish to come into your life. That is the job of the universe alone. Just take the energy

and the good feeling with you into your day after this meditation.

For the manifestation of your wish to work, your frequency must match the frequency of your fulfilled wish, so you must always take and feel the energy of what you wish for. This is also how you can easily tell if you are lacking in certain things. Your emotions are your feedback system here, because they are closely related to your thoughts. Dr. Joe Dispenza explains it this way: every thought triggers a biochemical reaction in your brain that causes your brain to send out certain chemical signals. These chemical signals cause a feeling in your body that matches that thought exactly. This feeling, in turn, causes even more thoughts of the same kind to arise, which leads to even more chemical signals that the feeling has already caused. What is created here is a thinking-feeling loop.[22] If you are inattentive, this can result in an infinite loop that determines your thinking and your feelings.

Where your attention goes, energy flows. Therefore, ask yourself again and again how you feel to make sure that you are "vibrating correctly". Do you feel full of joy about your manifestation? Or are you feeling a lack and thinking not of your fulfilled wish, but of the opposite and of what you don't possess at the moment? Your feelings tell you if you are open to having your wish fulfilled. Use this feedback system regularly and make it your daily principle to feel good and thus consciously resonate with your wish. As long as you focus on what you do NOT want, what you do want cannot come to you. But if you mainly think about the fact that your wish has already been fulfilled and you feel good, you can be sure that your wish is on the fastest way to you right now. For a change, play through not the worst-case scenario, but the best-case scenario, and thus break the continuous loop of negative thinking and feeling. Inspire positive thoughts and a good feeling by imagining what could happen in the best-case scenario. What could happen that would make you do a happy dance?

New wishes don't yet have the same power as thoughts of long-held wishes. If you do the *Energy Pulls* exercise as often as possible, you increase the frequency with which you send out super powerful frequencies and can give your manifestation an extra boost. The fact is, things you hold in your consciousness long enough are bound to manifest in the outer world. Earl Nightingale said, "*We become what we think about most of the time.*" If you want to change something in your life, you must start by changing your thoughts. If you increase the power with which you radiate the frequency of your manifested wish with your thoughts and do this as often as possible, you will receive the frequency of your fulfilled wish back with speed. The universe will manifest your wish as fast as possible – because what you want, wants you too.

"Creation is always happening. Every time an individual has a thought, or a prolonged, chronic way of thinking, they're in the creation process. Something is going to manifest out of those thoughts."

-– Michael Bernard Beckwith

2.4

"Ask and you shall receive" – ask the right questions!

You can change all things if you ask a question. Even in the Bible it is written that if you ask, it will be given to you. *"Ask and you shall receive"* or *"Ask and it shall be given you"*. In fact, these are not words that come easily and mean little. I have found that the universe answers *all* the questions you ask. ALWAYS. It's just a matter of you learning to ask the right questions. Because every question, every request and every wish has a certain energy. With every question you ask, you send out a certain frequency and draw the corresponding frequency into your life. Questions are thus, along with your energy and intention, another important key with which you can manifest your wishes. Intentions work, but questions work better because they are like door openers. Questions create possibilities. Answers, statements and definitions, on the other hand, create limitations to what is actually possible.[23] Most of the time, you would never have come up with such a great answer yourself as the universe can give you. Your brain only knows answers based on the knowledge and experiences you have had so far in your life. If you want a quantum leap in life, use the technique of asking the right questions.

So, what is the difference between intentions and questions? Is one better than the other? You can think of it as ordering at

59

a restaurant. You can either ask, *"Can I please have the zander in dill sauce?"* or you can say, *"I would like the zander in dill sauce."* One is an intention and the other is a question. Both will work and get you the order you want, as long as you're sure you really want the zander in dill sauce. If you're unsure if it's the best thing for you at that moment or you're not sure what you want, ask a different question, such as *"Can I please get the healthiest dish from the menu?"* or *"What are the infinite ways that I can get the healthiest dish for me and my body from this menu?"*

Have you ever noticed yourself asking *"Why does this always happen to me?"*, *"Why did this happen?"* or *"Why did he do that?"* when something bad happened? Such questions are not the right ones if you want to create miracles. All these why questions don't go unanswered by the universe. However, it only shows you more of what you don't want to have and you energetically attract more of such situations into your life that lead to what you actually don't want. So, it's about asking powerful questions. Powerful questions are really a great manifestation tool. Instead of setting an intention in your morning meditation or even at some other time during the day, just ask a question to the universe.

Any situation in your life that needs to change is perfect for asking questions to the Universe. Questions always open up possibilities. Live in the question. The more questions you ask, the more opportunities you give the Universe to deliver to you what you truly desire. Basically, asking questions works like the *Energy Pulls* exercise in Chapter 2.3. If you consciously send out the frequencies that correspond to love, joy, prosperity, you will draw these frequencies into your life. What energy do you want to attract? What questions can you ask?

For example, Vishen Lakhiani, founder of *Mindvalley*, speaker and bestselling author asks the Universe the following questions:[24]

- Why am I always surrounded by happiness and joy, no matter what?
- Why am I always surrounded by love and great people with whom I feel a deep connection?
- Why am I so brilliant and such a genius and why do I find it so easy to connect with my creative power to find inspiration immediately?
- Why do I achieve my dreams and goals with such ease and speed?
- Why does the universe always have my back?
- Why can I get so much done in such a short amount of time?
- Why am I so good at making money, saving it too, and multiplying it?

The right questions can help you create awareness of what experiences you want to experience. They can help you focus your attention on what you really want. So always ask open-ended questions to open yourself up to what you haven't seen before. Open yourself to the answers that the universe will give you. And you can be sure that the universe will give them to you, you don't have to search for them or force them. The answers of the universe can be completely different than you might expect. Let yourself be surprised. The universe has much more in store for you than you can imagine – and likes to deliver more than once, as you've already noticed! Now it's your turn.

Exercise: Ask a question

What questions could you ask to manifest your desires with ease and speed? What questions could you ask to make your life better? Asking questions regularly is a great way to bring more magic into your life. Think in terms of questions and open the door to the universe. You can make a real routine out of it, for example by starting your day every morning with a question to the Universe.

Here's a list of questions to inspire you:

- What else is possible?
- How can things get even better right now?
- What miracle is waiting for me around the next corner?
- How can I have more fun?
- What will it take to make a difference?
- What if …
- Why am I so healthy?
- Why am I so rich?
- Why am I so grateful for my life?
- Why do I feel so loved by my partner?
- How can I be generous today?
- How can I give today?

- What can I do today to maximize my success?
- How does it get any better than this?
- Why am I so happy?

Did you ask your question? Now be excited for the wondrous ways the Universe will find to answer that question for you. To make sure you don't miss the Universe's answers, learn how to better interpret its language in Chapter 5.

> "That's the most important aspect of this.
> You've got to be willing to ask the question and go
> beyond your limited beliefs. The only way you're going to
> go beyond what you beli
> eve is by asking a question."
>
> — Gary M. Douglas

3.

Energetic blockages that sabotage your orders and how you can solve them

Why it doesn't always work out with manifesting can have various reasons. The wishes and goals we set for ourselves result from our perception of the outside world. But the perception of your outer world is limited by your own consciousness. Your consciousness develops and makes experiences depending on which stage of development it is on, as well as how successful it is with manifesting. As within, so without – this is also described by the hermetic laws in the Kybalion.

Often, we wish for things and set goals based on society's expectations that we believe are right for us. We wish for money, wealth, a job that gives us a good reputation – but all this might not be what your soul is calling for. Your soul probably has a very different plan for you and that's why sometimes manifesting your wishes just doesn't work out. Sometimes you wish for something, but it is not the right thing for you at the moment or something much better is waiting for you. Surely you have also experienced that in retrospect you were glad that you didn't get the job you applied for because you found a better one or that you didn't book the vacation to Hawaii but to Costa Rica where you met your current partner.

We can only set our goals based on what we already know. Our current knowledge is limited by our ego and mind, our society, our environment, our religion and the western world's definition of success. In fact, we know next to nothing about what our soul has intended for our lives.

Sometimes, however, manifesting doesn't work out perfectly because external life circumstances, other people, and entrenched beliefs create thoughts and emotions within us that can change our frequency and thus prevent us from successfully manifesting our wishes. Being able to control thoughts and emotions is indeed a true art. Events can occur that create inner dialogues and doubts within you that your wish will manifest. If you are unaware, such feelings and thoughts can actually sabotage your orders from the universe. To release such energetic blocks, a change of perspective is required to shift your frequency again. As Michael Beckwith, founder and director of the Agape International Spiritual Center, describes it, *"Problems that arise are a means of communication from the universe. When a problem arises, it does not appear alone, but with a question that wants to be asked. And each answer brings with it an action that wants to be taken. With each action, in turn, a new way of living wants to be awakened."* [31]

If problems arise in your life that cause suffering and loss, understand them as signals. The universe is talking to you and wants to show you that you are going in the wrong direction. Perhaps you are pursuing goals that you should not be pursuing. Maybe you are chasing dreams that are not meant for you. Something that is meant for you doesn't come with problems and stress. It just flows. What you really want, what your soul intended for you, also wants you. It's looking out for you and finding ways to enter your life. Acknowledge these signals as a gift, for they are the most powerful tools for your growth.

Thoughts of *how* the universe will deliver your order are also a hindrance, as they can create doubt in you. Imagine you wish to finally take a trip around the world, but you just don't have the financial means yet. You think to yourself, *"How can this wish come true? I don't have any money!"*. Such thoughts create a huge mountain of doubt in you. If you don't believe that you will get what you wish for, your order to the universe won't work. That's because doubt just attracts more doubt. You don't have to know how the universe will make it possible for your wish to come true. It will manifest your wish; all it needs is your trust. Give up control completely. You can't control the universe. Leave the *how* completely open, let go of the pressure. You also don't need to know *when* your wish will manifest. Just have faith that your order will be delivered at the right time, no matter how or when. The universe will take care of it! As soon as you send out the frequencies of your fulfilled wish, an insane number of small variables come into play – all of which you can't even begin to understand because they are beyond your imagination. Most of the variables are outside your field of vision. But you don't need to know these variables. Rely on the universe to move mountains to fulfill your wish. Leave it to the universe to find the best possible way to deliver your wish. It will attract the right people into your life and create situations and circumstances in your life that you cannot even imagine at this time. As long as you don't worry about the *how* and the *when*, everything will work out fine. What prevents the law from manifesting your wish is your doubts alone. Focus your thoughts on your already fulfilled wish and let it come to you.

Sometimes, however, through your wishes, you communicate to the Universe the very thing you don't want to manifest in your life. And this is always the case when you chase your wishes too much. By giving them too much importance, wanting to achieve something at all costs and telling yourself again and again and thinking that you really absolutely need this and that, you create a resistance and radiate the frequency that you don't have that in your life. Which in turn only draws more lack into your life. The universe likes to think up all kinds of things, after all, so many things vibrate on the frequency of lack. It delivers gladly one misfortune after the other. Maybe you experienced this already. And even if you keep thinking how nice it would be if you had already reached your goal, you might unconsciously go into the feelings of waiting and impatience, with which, however, you only manifest more waiting and impatience. Always be mindful of what frequency your antenna is tuned to. In order to bring your frequency into harmony with that of your wish in order to receive it, it is important that you dissolve such resistances. This works by not seeing your wish as something you have yet to achieve, but by seeing your manifested wish as already a part of you. Always be the energy of what you want to manifest. It is always about the energy!

Often our beliefs also prevent us from successfully manifesting our wishes. Beliefs are thoughts that you believe in really strongly and therefore manifest. A good example is money. Our thoughts around money are often negatively polarized. Many people believe that it is hard to earn money, that you have to work a lot to earn a lot of money, or that it is bad to have a lot of money and so on. Such beliefs can only take you further away from financial prosperity. Your beliefs are nothing more than stories you tell yourself because you believed them somewhere at some point. Most of them actually date back to childhood years and are buried deep in your subconsciousness. This is actually a piece of work to track down and reprogram these little buzzkills. If you want to attract money, you need new beliefs like *"I am worth having a lot of money"*, *"Making money is fun"*, *"Making money is easy"* or *"I always have a lot of money"*. I have tried many techniques to find limiting beliefs. When I took on the topic of money with myself and dissolved probably hundreds of beliefs about this topic, my income tripled within 6 months. I grew up in a working middle class family and you wouldn't believe how much social and societal programming there was, which clearly got in the way of making more money than my parents. I've heard similar stories from many successful people who instead of marketing, focused on mindset coaching and gave their attitudes and views about money a software update. So, you don't have to spend as many hours doing this as I did, in the next chapter I'll show you a technique I learned from mindset coach Vanessa Simpkins that makes detecting these little buzzkills easy and fast with the support of your intuition.

"You attract to you the predominant thoughts that you're holding in your awareness, whether those thoughts are conscious or unconscious. That's' the rub."

— Michael Bernard Beckwith

3.1

How to reprogram limiting beliefs in minutes instead of years

Is there sometimes a voice inside telling you not so helpful things like *"I'm not good enough"*, *"I'm not worth it"* or *"I have to do everything on my own"* or *"I don't know what to do"*? These are all limiting beliefs that come from your subconsciousness and they can be real buzzkills. They are nothing more than stories that you consistently tell yourself – although unconsciously – and are reflected in your outer world. You may not even know all the beliefs that are keeping you from living to your full potential. *"It's hard for me to loose weight,"* *"It's hard for me to make money,"* *"I'll never find the right partner for me"* – these beliefs keep you trapped. If you haven't gotten to where you'd like to be financially, or if you still don't have what you'd want in your life, it's 100% because of your beliefs.

Changing these actually requires looking inward to find out what negative beliefs are floating around in your subconsciousness that are holding you back. If you want to break free from your limiting beliefs, you first need to locate them and then reprogram them. You need a software update, so to speak!

Let's do a little thought experiment. What would happen if you actually failed to reach your goal of earning X amount or starting your business? What is the worst thing that could happen? You would lose everything? What would that feel like?

Really immerse yourself in what it would feel like if you blew it all. What does that feeling feel like? Your ego is always there to protect you and it does so with fear. The feeling you're feeling right now has emerged from a thought from your subconsciousness. You can get rid of this feeling with another thought. Because another thought creates another feeling in you.

If you are aware of the stories you tell yourself, you can change them. To find them, you just have to ask the right questions. All the answers are there, but they lie beneath the surface, hidden in your subconsciousness. Now to find them, answer the following question without thinking. The following formulations are aimed at the same question, to draw out the hidden belief with the help of your intuition. Get really quiet and take some deep calm breaths before you do this exercise undisturbed.

- *What do I believe about myself or my life that created the (problem) that is currently showing up in my reality?*

- *What thought am I secretly thinking that created what is currently showing up in my life?*

- *What must I be unconsciously thinking about myself or my life to have manifested the (problem/situation)?*

- *What view do I have about myself or my life that created this?*

What is the first answer that pops into your head? This is your core belief. It is impossible for your external world to be different from your core beliefs. But once you are aware of your core beliefs and the stories you tell yourself, you can change them. There are many tools available to change beliefs. Maybe you already have experience with them and know how to do it? At this point I will explain you a simple technique that you can use and that works if you have no further experience with reprogramming beliefs. I personally use the Clearing Statement from *Access Consciousness* (https://www.accessconsciousness.com/theclearingstatement). Be aware though, it is not so much the tool you use to reprogram, but your conscious choice to think a new thought now. You can easily strengthen this thought with affirmations, which we will discuss in more detail in the next chapter.

Exercise:
How to reprogram your limiting beliefs

Take a few of your limiting beliefs and write them down one by one. If you can't think of any off the top of your head, take a situation and a topic and uncover the limiting beliefs that come up about it using the exercise on the previous page. Next to each of your limiting beliefs, write down the opposite belief. *"I can't do this"* becomes *"I can do this"* and *"I am not good enough"* becomes *"I am perfect the way I am"*. Usually, your intuition gives you new right beliefs. It is important that you formulate your beliefs effectively, i.e., in the present tense: *"I am"* instead of *"I will..."*.

Some ideas for powerful affirmations:

- I am good the way I am
- I love myself

- I am a winner
- I can have absolutely anything I want

To reprogram your subconsciousness mind as quickly as possible, repeat your new beliefs several times a day. Repetition is the key to efficiently reprogramming your subconsciousness and changing your frequency. Another success factor is visualizations that you can combine with your new beliefs.

Exercise: Mindmovie – Visualize the affirmation

What do you want to achieve? Imagine in detail what will happen when you have already achieved this goal. What are you doing? Where are you? What can you hear? See these events through your eyes and experience the situation with all your senses. Create a small movie in your mind's eye, lasting about 30 seconds. Feelings are the key point. Add a special moment to your 30-second movie: someone close to you, your life partner, your daughter or your son hugs you and praises you for what you have achieved and tells you *"I am so proud of you"*. This feeling is the extra boost and will reprogram your beliefs at the speed of light! Play this little movie over and over again in your mind's eye. As many times as it takes until you live the reality in which you have accomplished what you want.

> "Whatever the human mind can imagine and
> believe in, it can accomplish!"
>
> — Napoleon Hill

73

3.2

Affirmations – Train your Mind

A new belief you want to program in is nothing more than an intention. You're probably yawning right now because everyone is always talking about affirmations, but it's really important that you know how and most importantly, that they work. Affirmations are really everything you say and think. They are the voices in your head that speak to you and influence your frequency. Much of what we normally say and think is not really positive and does not create positive experiences. Whenever you complain about something, that is an affirmation. If you want to experience positive changes in your life, change negative speech and thought patterns into positive ones. Choose your affirmations consciously to trick your brain, reprogram your subconsciousness and create your new identity. Affirmations bring you into the feeling that what you wish for is already there and are a powerful tool you can use to clearly tell the Universe what you want so there are no misunderstandings!

Oftentimes, we say and think things like *"I don't want that in my life"* instead of communicating to the Universe what we actually want to have. *"I hate this job"* will not create the experience you wish for. Affirmations really work if you phrase them correctly. Use all your senses when you formulate your affirmations, say them to yourself, write them down, and listen to them (you can find numerous audio files and videos of affirmations on the web, for example by Louise L. Hay).

- **I Am Affirmations**: Affirmations that you begin with *"I am"*, such as *"I am healthy/happy/rich/ in love..."* are especially powerful and transform your frequency to the frequency of what you want to manifest.
- **Affirmations in the form of questions to the Universe**: such as *"Why am I making a million dollars with my business?"*

To experience what you wish for, state your affirmations clearly. Focus on the result you want to achieve, not the process by which you get there. You want to lose a few kilos and finally be sporty and fit? Then the ideal affirmation for you would be, *"I live like someone who is super athletic and fit."* How would a person feel who is athletic and fit? Give your affirmation an extra boost of energy by immersing yourself in the corresponding feeling, thus vibrating at the frequency of a person who is super athletic and fit. You will then attract all sorts of frequencies that match that. The universe will send you multiple experiences and situations that will make you athletic and fit. You will probably notice foods in the supermarket that support this attitude towards life. You will feel motivated to wear sporty clothes and go to the gym and maybe you will meet your new workout buddy there, with whom going to the gym will be much easier for you right away.

It's best to choose three Power-Affirmations that support the wish you want to manifest and incorporate them into your day. Immerse yourself in the energy of these three affirmations as often as possible to receive a quick delivery from the universe.

You may have been carrying your negative affirmations for a long time. Eliminating these thoughts from your life and creating new ones is a process that requires a little patience. Louise L. Hay says, *"Affirmations are like seeds you plant in the ground. First, they germinate, then they sprout roots, and then they shoot up through the ground. It takes some time to go from a seed to a full-grown plant. And so it is with affirmations – it takes time from the first declaration to the final destination. Be patient."* [32]

Michael Beckwith recommends taking a little time each day to work on new affirmations and pair them with visualizations and the feeling you feel when you manifest your goal. As you write down your affirmations, more limiting beliefs and things may come up in you that want to be resolved. With this process, your body cleanses itself. You can embrace this process because it changes your frequency to the one that will lead you to your goal.

By the way: Positive thoughts are many times stronger than negative thoughts, because the accompanying feeling has a higher frequency (see chapter 3.3). So, you don't have to be afraid of negative thoughts, and you don't have to fight them or suppress them. If you just accept that they are there and don't fight them, you won't lose as much energy to them and it will be much easier for you to let them go. Focus your energy on your positive affirmations. Bring light to your past and the resulting beliefs that prevent you from using your full potential. When you believe in yourself again, step into your power and change your self-image, you will be able to manifest even more successfully. With spiritual growth, you will become who you really are. And remember, you are always just a thought away from a new life.

"The thoughts we choose to think
are the tools we use to paint the
canvas of our lives."

 — Louise Hay

3.3

More energy, more miracles – how to raise your frequency

When manifesting, your energy plays the main role. The frequencies you send out determine what you attract into your life. And since the Universe is so happy to deliver anything that matches the frequency you are sending out, it is so important that you are mindful of what frequencies you are transmitting. How you feel right now in this moment directly affects your outer world. Positive emotions such as gratitude, joy and bliss have a particularly high frequency, as described by scientist David Hawkins in his study[33] on levels of consciousness that he published in the late 1990s (see chart on page 79). Negative emotions are the biggest saboteurs when it comes to using your full manifestation potential. Emotions such as sadness, guilt, anger, rage, or shame resonate very low. Such emotions keep us stuck in flight-or-fight mode and cause us and our bodies constant stress, as Hawkins explains. These emotions go hand-in-hand with a victim mindset and produce negative thoughts on top of that, which sends you right into the negative thought-feeling loop. Negative emotions from the lower levels of our conscious states, such as fear, cut off the connection to your creative power. Fear is a natural protective program of your ego that becomes active when you feel insecurity. But it's also the exact opposite feeling of joy and confidence. These are absolutely not the feelings you need to manifest. To connect with your creative power, you need feelings from the upper skala.

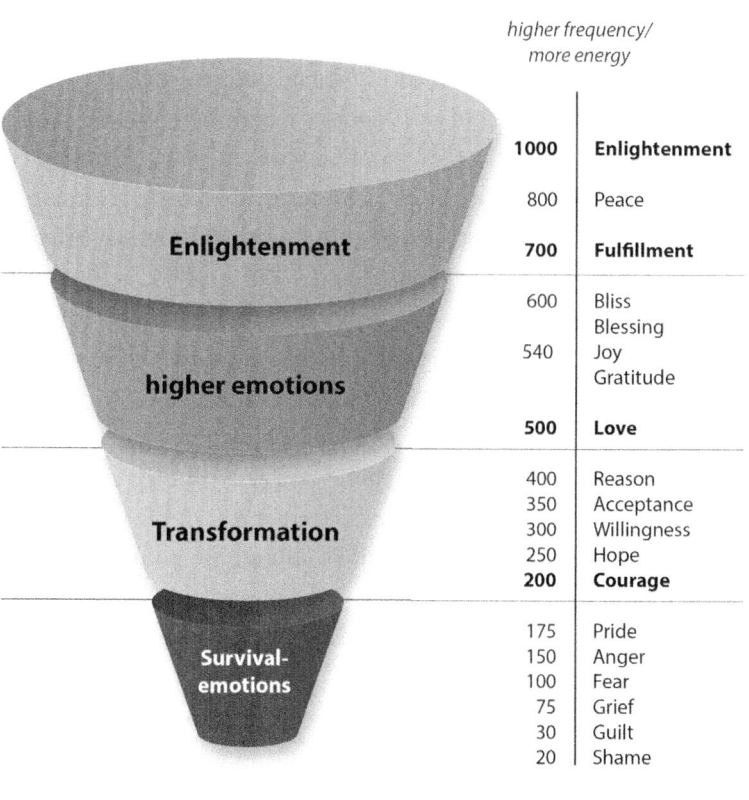

higher frequency/
more energy

1000	**Enlightenment**
800	Peace
700	**Fulfillment**
600	Bliss
	Blessing
540	Joy
	Gratitude
500	**Love**
400	Reason
350	Acceptance
300	Willingness
250	Hope
200	**Courage**
175	Pride
150	Anger
100	Fear
75	Grief
30	Guilt
20	Shame

slower frequency/
more matter

The Map of Consciousness by David Hawkins
(adapted from https://de.spiritualwiki.org/Wiki/Consciousness-Tables)

Unfortunately, we humans are downright addicted to feelings of fear. Charles Darwin discovered that the feeling of fear is an automatic reaction of the body to an external threat – whether real or imagined. In Neanderthal times, fear helped us survive and was a feedback system as to what was safe and what was not. Fear is deeply ingrained in us, but unfortunately these reflexes no longer fit into our modern world. Perhaps you have noticed that we quite often manifest what we are actually afraid of. Fear and doubt usually go hand in hand. Your fear actually only wants to warn you of something. In the future, pay attention to how you react to your feelings of fear. If you react with doubt and worry, you will attract what you are afraid of into your life. However, if you act constructively with consideration for the fear and approach it with small courageous steps, you can dissolve it.

We often don't trust that things can go well for any length of time. Author Gay Hendricks, describes this in his book *"The Big Leap"* with the **Upper Limit Problem,** the point at which your subconscious mind creates new dramas because you subconsciously don't believe you deserve this much happiness, joy or wealth.[34]

It's important to believe that you will attract good things into your life with ease. So many more wonderful things can come from this belief set. It will be much easier for you to keep your energy frequency at a higher level of consciousness. You can make the choice to feel good at any moment. When you feel good, you have direct access to your creative power. Remember: high frequencies have more energy and therefore help your miracles to come to you faster.

We all have bad days and feel grim, tired, unbalanced or annoyed. That's perfectly okay, that's absolutely human, you don't need to judge yourself for that. If you're having a bad day, it's perfectly okay to allow and accept those feelings. However, try not to let the negative feelings get the upper hand and control you and your state of mind. Even small activities can make you feel better and raise your frequency again. Do something that feels good to you. Keep going, even if you don't have as much energy on this bad day.

It's easier than you think to feel good again! What makes you happy and gives you more energy? It can be simple things like spending time in nature, listening to your favorite song, singing, cooking your favorite dish, spending time with your loved ones, dancing … Whatever puts you in a good mood and gives you an energy boost – do it! Things that make you happy transform your frequency into the exact frequency you need to manifest your wishes. And with that, you'll attract more situations back into your life that match the frequency of happiness.

Tips to increase your frequency:

- Get out in nature and move around a bit.
- Catch some sun! When sun shines on our skin, we absorb vitamin D, which brings feelings of happiness to us and is guaranteed to lift our mood.
- Give yourself a break from social media and be offline more often.
- Do something good for your body and drink plenty of water to keep yourself hydrated. Sometimes we simply don't drink

enough, which can cause emotional imbalance. Drink clean water with minerals.

- Eat something that is healthy for your body. Foods that are as natural and as unprocessed as possible. Organic fruit, for example, provides a tremendous amount of vital energy. It also makes a huge difference in terms of nutrient content whether you eat cooked or fresh vegetables. Also avoid artificial sweeteners, these substances prevent your brain from thinking clearly. Eat foods with a high vibration (organic vegetables and fruits), eat vegetarian and healthy.

- Take a few deep breaths. Breathe in oxygen, pure life force, and revitalize your cells with fresh energy.

- How about a dose of self-love in the form of a warm bubble bath, delicious chocolate, a hug from your loved one, your favorite movie, a new dress or fresh flowers?

- Move more, exercise!

- Cleanse your body of metals and toxins (colon cleansing, detox juice fasting).

- Use only natural remedies for everyday ailments like headaches or fatigue (ginger, peppermint, fresh air, exercise, …).

- Free yourself from addictions (cigarettes, caffeine, alcohol, drugs).

- Do regular exercises to ground yourself, such as breathing exercises, meditation, walk barefoot in nature.

- Be grateful. The feeling of gratitude resonates on a very special frequency. When you feel feelings of gratitude, you attract more events into your life to be grateful for. If you feel bad, you can easily change your frequency with gratitude and feel better.

- Bless everything and everyone all the time! Don't forget to bless yourself!

Sometimes little sleep or a lack of nutrients can also be responsible for us feeling bad and having little energy. It's best to have your family doctor check you out and make sure you are getting enough of all the important nutrients. Your health and well-being have a huge impact on your frequency. Always take care of your body and make sure that you feel well. Even with very simple tools you can bring your frequency to a higher vibration and get more energy. And more energy means more miracles!

Exercise:
When you find yourself in a negative thoughts spiral …

Sometimes, we get into a spiral of negative thoughts when something unexpected and unpleasant happens in our lives. But contrary to what it may seem at first glance, difficult times bring a lot of good, because they create clarity where there was none before. You again have attracted a partner into your life who is always working, pays little attention to you and spends little time in your relationship? Negative events and problems bring you clarity about what you want to have instead. For example, a partner who values you and is there for you. Negative events are a gift from the universe because they help you grow. Embrace them. You don't have to try to change your whole life to feel better. You don't have to do much at all. Gabrielle Bernstein, best-selling author and spiritual teacher, has designed a 3-step technique you can use if you find yourself lost in a negative thought spiral.

The "Choose Again Technique"[35]

1. **Become aware of your thoughts:** Is everything going haywire and are negative thoughts buzzing around in your head? Negative thoughts and unhappiness are like alarm bells ringing to alert you to them. They don't resonate on the frequency of what you want to attract into your life. If you become aware of your negative thoughts, just notice them without judging them. Ask yourself how you feel in that moment.

2. **Don't judge yourself for your thoughts:** Don't judge yourself, but forgive yourself for putting your focus in the wrong direction. Accept the situation and feel gratitude for this gift from the universe that shows you what you don't want to have in your life. You can deepen the feeling of gratitude by saying to the Universe, *"Thank you dear Universe for making me aware of what I don't want in my life, to give me clarity about what I do want."*

3. **Choose again:** Ask yourself what is the next best feeling you can feel right now, in this moment. Then ask the universe to show you the way: *"Thank you, dear universe, for showing me the way to my positive feelings."*

When you think of the good feeling you want to feel right now, don't try to make big jumps, just focus on the next best feeling. Trust the universe to help you feel better again and listen for the new thought it gives you. You just have to ask for it!

Exercise: Spiritual guidance from the spiritual world

Another way through which you can get out of the negative thought spiral is through prayer. You can always ask the spiritual world for help and spiritual guidance. This can be angels or the holy spirit. There are 7 little words with which you can unhinge any problem. Feel free to try it out, for me this prayer has sometimes worked wonders overnight.[36] You can say it a few times in a row and you may find the next morning that the problematic thought has vanished into thin air or your issue is no longer weighing you down quite as much.

> *"Dear Holy Spirit,*
> *please heal all my fear-based thoughts."*

This is the basic prayer, but you can expand it to include your issue, for example, *"Please heal my fear-based thoughts about my self-worth so that I can experience the true love I deserve."* You can apply it to any fears or negative thought spirals you're upset about.

The learning process always starts with becoming aware of the negative thoughts, but not judging for them. Where the negative thoughts actually come from and what the real purpose is, you will learn in the next chapter.

"Prayer is the medium of miracles."

— A Course in Miracles

3.4

Spiritual Ninja Growth – How to completely dissolve energetic blockages, fears and negative thoughts

Honestly, how many useless and negative thoughts run through your head every day? Would you like to mute the chatter in your head if you could? Most of them are thoughts that your brain, or rather you, don't create, but that your mind thinks on Autopilot. So that voice in your head that never stops chattering and sometimes thinks the stupidest thoughts, and usually on continuous loop, makes up 95 % of your thoughts? Not so cool, is it? Why does the mind do that? Have you ever wondered where those negative thoughts actually come from? As we remember, everything is energy, thoughts are energy. These negative thoughts are energy that got stuck in your system. They came about because you didn't like an experience you had. You didn't let the energy flow through you, you went into resistance. The same thing happens when you like something too much in life and you definitely don't want to loose it. The chatter in your head is all that blocked energy inside you that just wants to get out, like those old tea kettles that start whistling and rattling under pressure.[37]

You actually have to use your willpower all the time to keep that energy in and push it back down. We all know suppressed feelings, don't we? Suppressed thoughts from every millisecond throughout your life about all the events that didn't suit you are trying to discharge here. Do you know the feeling, when you're seething inside like a volcano because you're angry? This is energy that has accumulated and wants to be discharged. So don't get mad at yourself the next time you find yourself thinking so much "crap" again. It's really just accumulated "crap" from your whole life that wants out. Michael Singer calls it your samskara. **Samskara** in Sanskrit means *"a blockage, and impression from the past. It's an unfinished energy pattern that ends up running your life."* [38] All the psychology techniques will be able to explain this to you. Your entire reality in the now is created through the not so rose-colored glasses of your experiences gathered in the past. By the way, if you wake up some nights and have had another crazy dream, it is simply all the samskara that your mind or subconsciousness was able to release and process in the dream because it is "free" while you are asleep. So next time you can even be happy if you had a bad dream because it means that your mind was able to get rid of some of your samskara and released the blocked energy.

Energy flows through your whole body, you are an energy being. The energy (life energy, chi, prana) flows from the lower chakra, from the root chakra, always upward through all seven chakras out into the universe through the crown chakra. You are always energetically connected to the earth and the universe. The reason energetic blockages occur in your energy flow is because of all the experiences in the outside world that you didn't want to endure, that you suppressed or held onto. When your life energy, your chi, encounters such a blockage, it manifests as the thoughts and feelings that go with it. These energetic blockages hinder the flow of energy in your system so much that you no longer express yourself to the outside, that is, your authentic self, but your self that is colored by your problems or preferences, but which are all based on your past. You can't help but manifest your past over and over again. This is also why Dr. Joe Dispenza's retreats are 7 days long. He wants people to manage to break out of the hamster wheel of their past and get into the habit of new thoughts and frequencies by getting away from their usual daily life.

Michal Singer explains this process, that is how thoughts and feelings arise in your system, in his book or online course *"The Surrender Experiment"*.[39] He kind of reminds me of a giggling Einstein, but he manages to explain all these things in an amazingly easy to understand way. He offers a very simple technique of putting an end to the dilemma of negative thoughts. It is a spiritual growth process, but the only solution to solve these problems once and for all, he says.

Exercise: Relax and Release[40]

1. Observe the negative thought. You are not your thought; you are the essence observing how you think that thought. Get into the observer position.

2. Observe the feeling that accompanies this thought. Be it fear, jealousy, envy, observe how or where these feelings work in your body.

3. You just observe the "drama" like in a movie without it touching you. While you are observing, relax. Relax.

4. Just let go, now take a step back in your observer position and look down on the thought/feeling or watch it from a distance. In doing so, you give the energy the space it needs to discharge. If you are sensitive, you can even feel the energy rising inside you and wanting to get out. This is not always pleasant, because the original event was not pleasant, otherwise you would not have suppressed it. If your heart hurts or you need to cry, let it happen. That is the energy that is discharging.

5. If the thought and feeling is still there, repeat this process as long as it is necessary. Relax and release. This can be done in a short time like two breaths.

Sounds easy, but it is not. It is a lifelong process, but one that will bring you true spiritual growth and ultimately the freedom you wish for. Singer says you should practice in everyday moments, such as the next time you get upset at the driver in front of you for going too slow or cutting you off.

After a while of spiritual clearing, when you start to feel the energy flowing through you again, it's an incredibly beautiful feeling. Only then, you really understand that you are truly an energy being. The more blockages you remove within yourself, the more energy can flow again and express itself in your life, as it does in the third level of consciousness. You naturally feel joy, happiness, love and even ecstasy in your everyday life. You feel full of energy and it doesn't matter who you love, what you do for work. You just feel good and inspired and everything seems to magically flow. From this level you can even manifest miracles very fast because the miracle energy that has been flowing in you since birth is now fully available to you. The spiritual teachers all tell the same thing: you must first do the inner work and get rid of your samskara if you want success and miracles in your life.

The teachings of Dr. Sue Morter, an expert in bioenergetic medicine, are based on a similar principle. She uses the Central Channel Breathing technique to show you how to use your breathing to allow energy to flow through your system, thereby clearing blockages. The breathing technique is part of the *"Energycodes"*, a system that shows how to consciously direct energy through your own body, clearing energy blockages in your chakras and body. Thousands of her patients report synchronicities and healing miracles that occur all by themselves as soon as the energy flows freely in the body again.[41]

You can get your energy flowing again in many different ways, be it through yoga, qi gong, meditation or energy work. From personal experience I can tell you that sometimes I almost have an orgasm of happiness when I see a particularly beautiful green in the forest and the colors of nature so intensely touch my heart. When you feel the energy flowing in your heart and everything becomes warm, you feel like you are being held by the universe. Also, when you are *pulling energy,* at some point you should notice how your heart opens and the area becomes warm. If it doesn't, you may have built up a **heart wall**. One of Dr. Bradley Nelson's most significant discoveries is that the body builds itself like a shield of emotions that close off your heart. It acts like a virtual wall as a protective function and is usually built up by the subconscious mind after emotional injuries.[42] I dissolved my heart wall a few years ago using the *"Emotion Code"*- Technique by Dr. Bradley Nelson.

As the energies flow from the bottom up, they go to the heart and trigger the appropriate feelings here, which communicate the energy blockages. The feelings, in turn, trigger the thoughts that are meant to alert you that there is an energy blockage. Michael Singer describes it this way, that the thoughts are rooted in the feelings. It's just a built-in feedback system that's supposed to alert you to that. I think through this technique we can learn to become more relaxed and stop wasting so much energy on unimportant things. *"Relax and release,"* as Singer says. Live in the moment!

"The root of the mind is at the heart."

— Michael Singer

4.

Train your Magical Superpowers – *Manifesting Hacks* for those in a hurry

Successful manifesting is something that requires regular practice. It's much like training muscles at the gym. If you want to build muscle, you need to exercise regularly. Manifesting also requires regular practice – it's kind of like the *Spiritual Gym*! The more you practice, the more powerful frequencies you will send out and the faster your wishes will be realized. There is no other way. And once you've learned to manifest, you can't unlearn it. This superpower will stay with you forever. It's like riding a bicycle.

In this chapter, I'll give you *Manifesting Hacks* to put in your toolbox for you to try out if you like. Test what you enjoy and keep what works for you.

Tool #1: Meditation

Meditation is the most powerful tool to connect yourself to your creative power. By meditating regularly, you strengthen your ability to better perceive your intuition. When meditating you calm your mind and can listen to your inner voice, your intuition. It cannot be explained with the mind, you can only experience it. Your intuition is your own personal GPS. It speaks to you to show you the way. However, it speaks to you in a quiet voice that you can hardly perceive if you don't listen carefully. Your intuition unlocks your creative potential, your true being. If you meditate regularly, you will find a better access to your intuition and you will be able to make it a part of your daily life. My tip: Meditate at least 10 minutes a day!

Tool #2: Manifest even faster with this breathing technique

If you send out stronger frequencies with your brain, you will be able to attract your wish faster. With this ancient Far Eastern breathing technique[25], it is possible to amplify the power of your frequencies through your breath alone to manifest your wishes faster. The built-in breathing pauses are the key points here, because they amplify your thoughts many times over, because your body absorbs life energy in the breathing pauses. You can combine this breathing exercise with meditation to harness the full energy of your body for your manifestation.

1. Inhale for 4 seconds.
2. Then hold your breath for 8 seconds.
3. Breathe out for 8 seconds.
4. Hold your breath for 4 seconds.

Repeat the exercise for several minutes. Try not to focus too much on counting, but rather try to create a natural breathing rhythm and visualize your wishes during the process. If you are using this technique for the first time, it might be a bit difficult for you to perceive this unusual breathing rhythm as normal and to focus on your visualization. But the more you practice, the easier it will be and the better you will be able to focus on what you want to create.

Tip: You can also use this breathing technique when you want to reprogram your beliefs. By thinking new affirmations repeatedly during this exercise as you breathe in and out, these new beliefs will enter your subconscious mind more quickly.

Tool #3: Decision making

Make a habit of talking to the universe and improving your relationship. You know that feeling of being faced with a decision and not being completely sure which choice is the right one? Actually, you know the answer, it's within you. Listen to your intuition. If you ask, you will get an answer. Here's a tool I learned from Dr. Dain Heer of *Access Consciousness*: ask, for example, *"If I make this choice, what will my life be like in 5 years?"* or *"What will my life be like in 5 years if I choose not to?"*. Listen to the feeling. Does it feel light and good? Or does it feel heavy? Light always means a "yes" is the answer from the universe. With these questions you have the opportunity to perceive the feeling that your choice will create. Some choices will give you a feeling of joy and lightness, others will give you a feeling of discomfort and heaviness. Always follow the path that gives you a feeling of joy and ease and you are guaranteed to make the right choice.

Tool #4: Visualization

A powerful tool that will help you activate your superpowers is to use the observer effect in the form of visualizing your goals in your mind's eye. This is because your brain can't tell if something is taking place in real life or if you're just imagining it. By regularly visualizing your goals, you can change your frequency and connect with the feeling that you have already achieved your goal.

However, visualization is by no means about just picturing your goal. That's why vision boards don't necessarily lead to success. Visualization is only a powerful tool if you do it right: the key is to change your perspective. As you visualize what you want to accomplish, look at the situation directly through your eyes, as if it were happening right now. Imagine yourself experiencing the situation. What can you hear or smell? Look around you at the moment you are reaching your goal and immerse all your senses in the energy of what you are experiencing. Let that feeling go into your body. How do you feel? What is your posture? What are you doing? What are you saying? Visualizing is basically just like shopping for new clothes to try on in the dressing room. You try on the clothes to know how they look on you and how they make you feel. It works the same way with visualizing the moment you want to manifest. Create the feeling of having already manifested your wish. Always be the energy of what you want to attract.

Tool #5: Raise Your Frequency with Gratitude

For this exercise, you will need something to write with.[26]

- Write down three things you are grateful for. For each thing you are grateful for, write down why you are grateful for it.
- Write down the names of three people for whom you are grateful. Also write down why you are grateful for each person.
- Ask yourself what part of these things you also have in you. Which of the characteristics or traits you just wrote down do you find in yourself?

Have you perhaps found traits and characteristics in yourself that you were not aware of before? Writing these things down is a brilliant exercise to find what you can be grateful for in yourself.

Tool #6: The Traffic Light Meditation

Your day offers you numerous moments to do short meditations, connect with your power and raise your frequencies to visualize your wishes. You don't even have to set aside extra time for this, because whenever you're standing in traffic at a stoplight waiting for it to turn green is an ideal moment for a little meditation.

The Traffic Light Meditation by the Silva Mind Technique[27] is a short meditation with eyes open and works like this:

1. Every time you stand at a red traffic light, change the focus of your gaze, let your gaze soften. You can keep your eyes on the traffic light, of course, but turn your focus inward.

2.   With your eyes open, visualize the wish you want to manifest.

3.   Direct your attention to your goals and feel the burning desire for your wish to manifest. Visualize yourself at the moment you have achieved your goal and briefly stay in this emotion.

4.   When it turns green, blink and redirect your focus to your outer world.

Open-eye meditations offer you the opportunity to give the manifestation process of your goals an extra boost several times throughout the day by connecting with the energy of your wish. Why not try the exercise now, you don't have to wait for the next red light. For example, I set my timer in my phone every hour for a while and briefly did the exercise when I wanted to manifest a short vacation. I always briefly imagined myself lying in the spa of my dream hotel. In addition, I pulled energy. A few days later there was a super great design hotel for 70 % discount, which looked almost exactly like my dream hotel and also not so far away. I booked right away. Thank you, dear universe :-)!

Tool #7: Dream Factory

Almost a third of the day we sleep. Time lost in which we could be working on manifesting our wishes? Not at all! You can use the time you sleep to realize your dreams (which you might actually dream about). In fact, your sleep is mainly responsible for manifesting your wish! A well-known technique[28] created by the famous spiritual author Neville Goddard to help you manifest your wishes faster describes how, in the twilight state, you immerse yourself in the feeling you feel when your wish is already fulfilled. By falling asleep with this feeling, your subconscious mind is reprogrammed. In the twilight state, between sleep and wakefulness, as in meditation, the subconsciousness can be shaped particularly effectively, because you are then in the alpha brainwave state.

The next time you are tired and lie down in your bed to sleep, try not to fall asleep immediately. When you enter a twilight state, ask yourself how you would feel if your wish was already fulfilled. What do you do and what do you think when your wish has manifested? Again, stay in the feelings of happiness or gratitude to the fullest. If you fall asleep with this feeling, it will have a direct influence on your subconscious mind. This is because your subconscious mind will not be able to distinguish whether these feelings are real or not. It accepts the truth that you feel to be true. By consciously reprogramming your subconscious mind with your feelings while you sleep, you will be able to observe changes in your external world and your wishes will manifest with ease.

Tool #8: Power Pose for Insecurity

Another way you can easily change your emotions is through your body. As your body pose changes, so do your thoughts and feelings. Research at Harvard University led by Amy Cuddy[29] has shown that a few minutes in a power pose – such as *Wonder*

Woman's (or Superman's) – can drastically change your emotions. This is because our muscles are connected to our brain. That's why you immediately feel happier when you smile. The muscles in your face automatically make you smile because they are connected to the emotional areas of your brain. It's not that you feel happy first and then think about smiling. When you're stressed, you frown or tense your shoulders – automatically. The whole thing also works the other way around: you can consciously evoke emotions with your body. That's probably why laughter yoga is so popular! Anyway, Amy Cuddy found that standing in a power pose for just a few minutes already increases hormones associated with self-confidence by 20% and lowers the stress hormone cortisone by 25%.

The next time you feel insecure or old beliefs like *"I'm not worth it"* or *"I can't do this"* come up, do a power pose, such as *Wonder Woman's*: put both arms on your hips and stand tall with both feet firmly planted in the ground. Be the energy of what you want to attract into your life. Be confident that you will achieve your goal. This exercise is great for starting your day with confidence.

Tool #9: Energy Transfer

This exercise is a great tool from Michael Beckwith's *Life Visioning process*[30] that you can use for areas of your life that are not yet in line with what you want. You can take the energy from an area of your life that is going great and where everything is in Flow and transfer it to a problem area to transform it. Take an area of your life or an event that makes you feel absolutely positive, where you are proud of yourself, what you have accomplished and feel into the emotions or high energy frequencies. Really turn up the frequencies, really feel into it so that your whole body is vibrating on that energy. Then think of the problem you want to transform while staying in the high energy frequencies. You are putting high energy frequencies on a lower frequency problem and helping it to vibrate higher. Feel great, while thinking about the problem, be sure to stay in the high frequency. By doing this, you are activating the high frequencies in that area. Now see what changes in your outer world over the next few days. Michael Beckwith calls this process *Energetic Shapeshifting*. Do this exercise every day until you see changes.

Tool #10: Ask your future self for advice

From Vishen Lakhiani, I learned a great technique to step into the frequency of your wish-reality:

1. Stand up and stand straight and relaxed. Imagine that you are about to step forward into your future self and become yourself in 5 years.

2. Now take one step forward. How do you feel? What do you see? Do you have any visions? Turn around, look back to your *present* self. What advice would you give your *present* self now?

Now sit back down and merge with your present self. What insights, visions or feelings did you have during this exercise?

"There is no hierarchy of difficulty
in miracles, for nothing is difficult
that is fully longed for."

— A Course in Miracles

5.

Hello Universe, can you hear me? Understanding the language of the universe ...

You diligently order from the universe, consciously send out the frequencies of your wish, regularly visualize your wish and work on reprogramming your limiting beliefs – but your wish just hasn't manifested yet? Of course, you're probably wondering why that is. How can it be that your wish still hasn't manifested? No need to worry, the universe has heard you. Everything you think and do leaves an energetic information in the quantum field. Have a little patience, some orders just take a little longer, because the universe knows no time. You experience a time delay only because all the frequencies you have ever sent out are still circulating and manifesting. Your thoughts from the past may therefore still be manifesting before your new thoughts have their turn. Don't give up when things manifest that you don't want to have. They are based on your beliefs or frequencies from the past. It can sometimes take a little while for the Universe to understand that you have changed your thoughts and begin to bring things into your life that are in alignment with your new frequency. The important thing is to keep your focus and not get rattled when unwanted events come into your life. Continue to ask powerful questions to the Universe such as, *"What can I do to be in the energy of my wish?"* or *"How can things get even better now?"* Don't get back into the victim mindset and ask yourself things as *"Why is this happening to me?"*, but rather recognize in problems an opportunity for growth. You can also do the following little exercise to not lose motivation.

Exercise: Universe, show me what I have already manifested

Often, we simply don't see what we have already set in motion because we are still waiting for the big result or something very concrete. Maybe you want to manifest earning X amount of money each month? It may take several steps to get there. In all likelihood, however, you are already on the direct path to your goal. Ask the universe clearly what you have already manifested:

"Universe, show me what I have already manifested!"

The universe will answer you and show you what you have already created and give you the certainty that you are on the right path. You want to earn 10,000 Dollar a month? Since the universe can provide you with anything that resonates at the frequency of your wish, it may not just deliver once, but send you the money in several small amounts rather than in one order. Or even quite differently than you expect. Maybe the universe has not only delivered money to you, but something that vibrates on the frequency of these 10,000 Dollars. This could be, for example, a great idea for a new business idea with which you can earn even more money in the future.

No question that you ask the universe remains unanswered. No wish goes unheard. The universe actually hears very well and it is super motivated to provide you with everything possible that matches the frequency of your wish. Sometimes it is just not so easy for us to see what we have already manifested, because so many things vibrate on the frequency of our wish. In addition, the universe does not speak the same language as we humans. It speaks in an energetic language that consists of signs, frequencies, synchronicities and mathematics. The universe speaks to you through situations, things, sequences of numbers, animals, plants, colors, and especially through your feelings and thoughts. If you have asked the universe a question or sent an order, be mindful of what is happening in your life, what events are occurring, what situations and people are coming into your life.

You may read something in the next few days that answers your question or that shows you how to manifest your wish. Maybe an animal keeps hanging around you and wants to bring you a message. Or you receive your answer in a dream. Also, numbers can give you information. Maybe you keep looking at the clock at the same time and see 11:11 or wake up at 4:44? Maybe your path overlaps with that of another person at a certain time (Completely by chance? There are no coincidences!), who gives you an important information or helps you further. If you had arrived at this place only half an hour later, you would never have met this person. Yes, the Universe is very fond of speaking in synchronicities because they catch our attention as they are different from ordinary life events. As soon as you notice more synchronicities, take it as a sign that you are on the right path. Everything that seems like a coincidence to you has a meaning. One of the great spiritual teachers, Wayne Dyer, dealt with the mysteries of synchronicity in his books for a long time. He says that when you understand synchronicity, you understand that the universe is actually alive and always working with you.[43] Synchronicities are always a sign that it is responding to your intentions, feelings and vibrations and resonating with you.

Sometimes, however, the message is quite small and inconspicuous, yet has great significance. Messages often also are hidden like a real treasure and are not apparent on the surface. Always be mindful, the messages can also be hidden inside. Ask yourself what is reflected in your outer world in response to the question you carry within. Sharpen your senses for the impulses you receive. What does your intuition tell you? Is it pointing you in a certain direction? Pay attention to the feelings you sense. They can also be your guideposts. The universe sometimes finds crazy ways to communicate with you. A shattered cell phone display can take on a whole new meaning. For example, the cell phone display can symbolize our perspective in life. If the display is broken, the universe may want to show you that you should dissolve an old view in your life that you may still be holding on to even though it has already shattered. Basically, everything carries information, everything can be a clue. Sometimes the universe means it really well with us and showers us with signs. Sometimes one misfortune seems to happen after the next, has that happened to you? The universe then calls to you: *"Hey! You have to change something if it is not to go on like this!"* and shows you in this way that you are not in resonance with your wish.

Sometimes it's just one word in a long list of emails in your spam folder that catches your eye and can change your day. I opened an email from my spam folder the other day and all I read was the word "Trust." Understanding the language of the universe can be a whole new way for you to encounter and interpret events.

"He who does not believe in miracles is not a realist."

 — Ben Gurion

6.

The Art of Manipulating Time – Applying Relativity Theory at home

Our perception of time is relative. Albert Einstein published the theory of relativity in 1905. He theorized that time passes differently in space than it does on Earth. An astronaut who has left Earth and flies around in space can return a century later, having aged only a little, and everyone he knew will have already passed away. The universe is a true mystery! Quantum physics shows that time, as we define it, basically does not exist. It is purely a human thought construct. Quantum physicists postulate that past, present and future run simultaneously. Quantum physicists showed in a strange space experiment with photons that a decision in the present can even change an event in the past.[44] Photons are what electromagnetic radiation is made of, which is why we also speak of light particles. Photons have the property of being able to behave like a particle or like a wave. In the famous observer effect[6] experiment it was already proved that an observer has influence on whether a photon behaves like a particle or like a wave. Now the physicist John Wheeler even found out that the photon could be influenced way earlier than the point in time when it either split like a wave or took a path like a particle.

The experiment proves that our ideas of the present, past and future are only mental constructs and all realities exist now, at this moment. And we humans like to hold on to our past: "*This happened to me then, that's why I am like this now*". But all this exists only in our memories. It is the same with our ideas about the future. We are so fascinated by the future and imagine the wildest things that could happen someday. But the future exists only as a potential in our imagination. Our ideas about the past and future are only concepts. All that exists is this moment. You alone are what you decide to be now, your past has no influence on it, as you may have believed so far. On the contrary, in the here and now you can even change your past and thus also your present and future.

Why am I telling you all this? You can absolutely use the knowledge about the relativity of time when making miracles. You can stretch time in your favor, you can get information from the future, travel into the past, delete parallel timelines and program yourself a new future. It all sounds wonderful, doesn't it?

Let's start with stretching time. You may know this, some people can stay calm in stressful situations under time pressure and get top notch results while doing it, whereas other people have absolutely no idea what to do first. Three minutes can be completely different depending on how you spend it. There are also huge differences in the perception of time between cultures. People in modern, industrialized cultures in the West, who are often under pressure and have full-time jobs, experience time very differently than natives of a Pacific Island, where time hardly seems to matter and everything is approached quite leisurely. Our perception of time is subjective. And we also have such different definitions of time, our personal perception of time and our own bio-rhythm. Sometimes we look at the clock every minute and time doesn't seem to pass at all, it really stretches. Sometimes it just flies away. And that's when we're in the flow, when we're busy and barely paying attention to time. Time actually seems to be more complex than we can even imagine.

Does your time often seem just too short? Your day is coming to an end, but you've only spent it working, commuting, and sleeping, but there's not much time left for you? The day has only 24 hours, we agree on that. But what if I told you that this day can become twice as long and you can have much more time? It works by stretching time. You can take ten minutes and turn it into what feels like an hour.

A well-known way that many well-known athletes already use to achieve a goal is to learn a new technique or instrument in your mind during a visualization. This way you can practice for an hour and do so within 10 minutes. After that, you'll make much faster progress in the "real" world and be able to implement what you've learned. This also works if you want to lose weight, if you want to break bad habits, or if you want to put more focus on a new project. You can do all of these things far more easily and in less of our measured time than usual.

A far lesser-known technique for stretching time works easily with your intention. Vianna Stibal, founder of *Theta Healing* says, *"Time is an illusion, a law of gravity that can be bent."*[45] You can even get nine hours of sleep in one hour with the following technique[46] from *Theta Healing*, if that's what you want.

Exercise: Stretching Time

With this exercise, you enter a dimension of time that allows you to stretch out a little time and experience it as much longer. You will be able to do all kinds of things in a short amount of time that would otherwise take you much more time.

1. Center yourself in your heart and connect with the universe. Close your eyes, notice your body, feel the boundaries of your body, where do you stop and where does the couch you are sitting on begin? Feel how your breath automatically flows in and out. Notice how you feel. Now feel yourself in all directions and imagine yourself expanding, first five feet in all directions. Up, down, left, right, back and forward. Now you expand 500 meters in all directions, then 1,000 kilometers. Then 10,000 kilometers. With each breath, feel your consciousness expanding until it encompasses the whole earth, and on and on. You are now as big as the galaxy, and with each breath you become lighter and bigger, as big as the universe itself. You are now infinite consciousness and one with the divine life force.

2. Now give the order to the Universe: "Dear Universe, I instruct that time is being changed by the Law of Time from the sixth plane of existence at this moment, on this day. I will have a restful sleep of 9 hours within one hour today. Thank you. It is done, it is done, it is done." *(as an example, change according to your needs)*

3. Witness (observe) in a brief visualization how the law adjusts the time according to your wish and your wish comes true. Through the observer effect, you make it real.

4. Thank again and finish the meditation.

You can use this for anything that comes to mind, such as when you think you're going to be late for work or an event because of slow traffic, or when you have a pile of work and need to get it done in just one day. Or even for nice moments when you want your vacation to feel longer.

It's also possible to go back to the past and change your experiences or simply erase mistakes and missteps of your life, which will directly affect your present and future as well. That sounds exciting, doesn't it? You can use the following exercise to enter parallel time dimensions where you can rewrite the script of your life and change both your past and your future.

Exercise: Time Travel with the Timeline Technique

Are there perhaps events in your life that you would like to change or even undo? With Time Line Therapy this is possible. It is a technique developed in the 1980s by NLP specialists Wyatt Woodsmall and Tad James that makes it possible to learn to understand and heal stressful feelings and to treat traumatic stress.[47] It is even possible to access resources that may have come from the future and thus can be brought into the present or past.

We humans usually store our memories chronologically (consciously or unconsciously), as if the events in our lives were strung together on a line. By imagining such a timeline, we can more easily organize the experiences in our lives and distinguish whether one event happens before or after another. Such a pictorial idea of the passage of time also helps us to distinguish whether we have already done a thing or intend to do it yet. And it is precisely this idea of the timeline that Timeline Therapy is based on, in which you make use of the metaphor of the timeline and enter an energetic field that connects you with the respective experiences from your past or future. In this technique you dive into the situation in the past where your problem is based and then resolve this event. You can use the Timeline Technique to undo experiences from your past that may have created negative limiting beliefs in you (*"I am not worthy"* or *"I am unimportant"*) and thereby dissolve these beliefs.

Travel back in time:

1. Think of an event in your past that you would like to change or a belief that you would like to dissolve. Get comfortable for this meditation, sitting or lying down. Close your eyes.

2. Now, in your imagination, float high above your head and imagine that you are looking at your timeline, forward and backward. Forward means the future and backward means the past. You may also visualize it from left to right or vice versa. Your subconsciousness is guiding you. From up here

you can move forward and backward on your timeline. Stop over the event in the past that is causing you the uncomfortable feeling and that you want to change or that is the cause of this belief. Your subconsciousness mind knows exactly where the right place is. Just trust your intuition.

3. Dwell on the event and notice the feeling. Ask yourself what positive experiences you were able to draw from this event. No matter how painful and bad the event has been in the past, it has also brought helpful and positive learning experiences.

4. Now float back a little further into your past, at least half an hour before the event occurred – when everything was still good. From there, look out toward the present into the future. Ask yourself where this feeling has now gone. You will find that it has disappeared. The stressful event has not yet taken place. If it hasn't disappeared yet, gradually let go of the stressful feeling and let it disappear, because you have already learned everything you could from that feeling. Visualize it dropping out of the timeline and disappearing upward into the universe.

5. Now do the test and immerse yourself in the experience in your timeline and check, if the feeling is still there. Then float back up above the timeline. Are there still remnants of the burdening feeling? If so, there may be more work to do. Perhaps there is an event further back in time that is causing

this feeling. In that case, go back to that time and start the process again.

6. Once the stressful feeling is neutralized, you can float back to the present, to the here and now, and open your eyes again.

Congratulations, you have just changed your past, your present and your future.

You can use the same technique when you want to manifest something. An infinite number of possibilities that you can imagine that can occur in the future already exist now. All realities exist simultaneously on a different frequency. And whether you are aware of it or not, you are wandering back and forth between the different realities. You can think of it as parallel timelines. With every choice you make right now, you're choosing a particular reality. Time travel is one of the coolest superpowers that people have and probably aren't even aware of.

The following exercise is inspired by Mindset Coach Regan Hillyer to program your future:[48]

1. Close your eyes and through a few deep relaxing breaths be aware that you are here now in this moment. You are in the present, your present reality. Breathe through your heart a few times and hold the intention of what miracle you want to bring into your reality now. Choose a date in your future by when you want it to manifest.

2. Now imagine that you are holding a small screen in your hands, and in the screen, there is a small movie showing how you are experiencing your miracle, how your wish is manifesting into the smallest detail. What do you see? What is happening? Who is in the film? What are the characters saying? Take a moment and watch this film. What details jump out at you? How do you feel?

3. On the edge of the screen, you will see buttons that you can use to adjust the brightness, color intensity, etc. You try the first button that changes the brightness. Turn it to "bright" all the way, then to "dark" all the way, and then choose the perfect brightness for your movie. Now turn the next knob to set the perfect colors. Turn it up so all the colors look like a cartoon, then turn it down so everything is like a black and white movie. And now adjust the knob so that your movie has the perfect colors for you. The third knob is for volume, you also turn it back and forth briefly and set a comfortable volume for the voices in your movie. The next button is for the intensity of the emotions. Turn it all the way up so that you feel all the strong emotions you would feel if your wish came true. And now turn it up even more, doubling your emotions so that you feel the joy throughout your body. Every cell in your body is vibrating, that's how strong your emotions are now. Triple the emotions!!!

4. Feel the whole screen vibrating that you are holding in your hands. Now jump into the screen so that you are in your

own movie. You experience your fulfilled wish with all your senses and through your own eyes. Store these feelings deep inside you. Jump out of the screen again and hold the vibrating screen in front of you again.

5. Energize the screen now with three breaths. Take a deep breath and with a loud "Ahhh" breathe all the life energy into the vibrating screen. Three times with all your power. Your whole body vibrates.

6. Now float high above your body with the screen in your hands and look at your timeline again. Be aware that you are floating above the now, then float into the future at the chosen time. Now hover over that point in time and drop the screen into that moment. Watch it fall into the timeline and suddenly everything adjusts. Look at your miracle moment and choose this as your new reality. It is done!

7. Now float back on the timeline into the now. Along the way, observe how timelines shift, fall away, and new ones are added. All the molecules in the quantum field adapt to your new chosen reality. Your future changes as you float back into the now.

8. You are now again floating above the now, looking into your future and feeling so much gratitude for your new reality and the miracle that is now programmed into your future.

Now let yourself sink back into your body and arrive back in the now and in your body. Take a deep breath. You have just changed your reality.

"The difference between past,
present and future is an illusion,
albeit a very persistent one."

– Albert Einstein

7.

The 21 Day Miracle Challenge

It's getting exciting, because now it's your turn. To help you train your superpowers, I'd like to invite you to a 21 Day Miracle Challenge. Research has shown that it takes an average of three weeks to replace an old habit with a new one. So now you have 21 days to reprogram your habits and make your brain realize that you have now gone among the miracle makers.

Every day for 21 days you will manifest small or big miracles by attracting the energy of your wish: new clients for your business, an invitation, money and much more! Once you are practiced, it will only take a few days or even just hours for your wish to come true. Even orders at Amazon don't arrive faster! We again use the technique of *energy pulls* to charge your intention with energy to the maximum and to give your miracle the necessary fuel.

Your daily orders to the universe follow the same pattern every day:

1. **Expansion meditation:** Center yourself in your heart and connect with the universe. Close your eyes and become aware of your body. Feel the boundaries of your body. Where do you stop and where does the couch you are sitting

on begin? Feel how your breath automatically flows in and out. Notice how you feel. Now feel yourself in all directions and imagine yourself expanding, first five feet in all directions. Up, down, left, right, back and forward. Now you expand 500 meters in all directions, then 5,000 kilometers. Then 100,000 kilometers. With each breath, feel your consciousness expanding until it encompasses the whole earth, and on and on. You are now as big as the galaxy and with each breath you become lighter and bigger. You are now infinite consciousness and one with the divine life force. You are the universe.

2. **Energy Pull:** Send your order to the universe with an intention or a question (see chapter 2.4). Now feel the energy of it. How would it feel if you had a magic wand and the wish had already come true? Form a ball of energy with your hands in front of your solar plexus chakra. Take the energy and fill the energy ball in your mind with the energy you would feel if you were to experience this wish come true right now. This could be pure happiness, joy and excitement. Put everything else you wish for into the energy ball. Now pull energy from the entire universe into this energy ball. You don't need to know exactly how this works. Just imagine in your mind how you attract energy from all directions and from above and below, which correspond to the same energy frequency. You feel the ball of energy in your hands expanding, filling with energy and getting bigger and bigger until you yourself are sitting in a big ball of energy. Keep pulling and pulling and pulling. Do this

quietly for a few minutes. When it gets warm in your heart, your heart is just opening up thanks to all the energy you are pulling into your energy ball and through you. When you feel tingling all over, send small beams of energy back into the universe to all the people, events and synchronicities that will help you bring your wish to fruition. Thank the Universe that your wish will come true with ease and as quickly as possible. That's it, let go of everything. Take the energy and the good feeling with you into your day after this meditation.

I have created a little diary for you, which you can use during your 21 Days Miracle Challenge. You will find a few blank lines for each day of your challenge. Write down every day when you placed your order with the Universe and ask yourself in the evening of your day what and when you manifested something. Write down any synchronicities you notice and thank the universe for the delivery.

Let's get started right now, today is Day 1 of your 21 Day Miracle Challenge. I recommend you always place your order in the morning.

Day 1

Today we start with something simple to warm up. Today you simply choose something that has a positive frequency and brings you great joy. It doesn't matter what. Leave it to the Universe to show you something beautiful.

Your order to the universe for today is for example:

"Dear universe, why does something positive happen to me today that I am very happy about? Please show me something beautiful today. Thank you so much, I'm looking forward to it!"

This is one of my favorite intentions to start my day with. It's an exciting game where you just let the universe do its thing. Every time, the universe shows me something that makes the day even better. And that strengthens my faith in the universe. With this intention, you give the universe the opportunity to surprise you in some way with something beautiful. Maybe it's a beautiful bird chirping or a magical sunset that the universe shows you. When you do the *Energy Pulls* exercise, at this point "just put something beautiful" into the energy ball and feel joy from something beautiful. Then pull the energy from all the frequencies that mean something beautiful to you.

What have you experienced?

_____

_____

_____

Day 2

Today you will manifest a message from a person you haven't heard from in ages. Try not to think of a specific person here, so as not to create expectations that might cause doubt. Just let the universe do it. This is a fun exercise. I suddenly received a message via Facebook from someone I must not have been in contact with for 8 years.

Tip: The delivery of your order can sometimes arrive 2–3 days later, because the universe knows no time. Sometimes it has to sort things out first and that can take earthly time. So don't worry if your order does not arrive today. In the energy ball, for example, you can visualize drawing energy from lots of people you haven't heard from in ages and sending little beams of energy back to them. You don't have to think of a specific person, pull energies from all directions. From behind usually means you are attracting something from your past, in front is the future, right and left mean people in general, above is the universe and below is the earth and everything you have built up so far and have already planted seeds for.

"Hello Universe, I am receiving a message from a person I haven't heard from in ages. I'm looking forward to the message. Thank you!"

What did you manifest?

_____

_____

Day 3

Today, you will manifest something fun. As you hold the energy ball in your hands, attract the energy frequency of joy and all things fun. Then see what happens today :-) …

"Dear Universe, why am I looking forward to having so much fun today? Great, thank you!"

What did you experience?

_____

_____

_____

_____

_____

_____

_____

_____

_____

_____

_____

_____

_____

_____

_____

_____

_____

_____

_____

_____

Day 4

We all love surprises, don't we? Of course, only those that make you happy. You too? Then just order one from the universe! When I was doing this exercise, the mailman surprisingly handed me a gift from a client that came in the mail as a thank you for my work.

"Hello dear universe, why did I receive such a great surprise which I'm so happy about? Thank you!"

What did you manifest?

Day 5

Do you like flowers? A fresh bouquet of flowers would look wonderful on your dining table, wouldn't it? Hmm ... Can you smell it yet? But maybe there are other things resonating on the frequency of flowers ... It could be a flowery smelling perfume. But anyway, let's let the universe do its thing!

"Dear universe, I'm receiving flowers today. Thank you so much, I'm looking forward to the great scent!"

What have you been experiencing?

_____

_____

_____

_____

_____

_____

_____

_____

_____

_____

_____

_____

_____

_____

_____

Day 6

Today you will attract the energy of courage, yes you heard right. It's time to be brave. Let's see what will happen, this wish allows for so many things! What have you not dared to do so far? Today, attract the energy of courage, adventure, self-confidence, bravery, self-love, justice and authenticity or simply courage as you dare :-).

"Hello dear universe. Why was I so brave today? Thank you for your support and for always having my back!"

What did you experience?

_____

_____

_____

_____

_____

_____

_____

_____

_____

_____

_____

_____

_____

_____

_____

Day 7

You get to enjoy a gift today, because you will get a gift. Gifts are a wonderful thing, especially when they come from the heart. Who do you think will sweeten your day? Only the universe knows. Let yourself be surprised! By the way, a miracle maker tried this out in a raffle at an event and then actually skimmed off one of the three prizes.

"Dear universe, why did I get a gift? I'm looking forward to it. Thank you so much!"

What did you get as a gift?

_____
_____
_____
_____
_____
_____
_____
_____
_____
_____
_____
_____
_____
_____
_____
_____
_____

Day 8

You have already completed the first week of your Miracle Challenge. Looking back, how did your week go? Did everything work out well? Did you attract things into your life that matched the frequency of your wish? Maybe there were some surprises and the result was completely different than you expected. But frequency is frequency! Your faith in the universe has probably already become a lot stronger. Now it is time to manifest your bigger wishes. For example, money. You will find some.

"Hello universe, I unexpectedly find money! Thank you very much, I am looking forward to my find!"

With me it happens quite often that I then find money on the street or unexpectedly in a jacket that I haven't worn for a long time. It is always exciting what the universe comes up with to deliver as quickly as possible.

How much money have you manifested?

_____

_____

_____

_____

_____

_____

_____

_____

_____

Day 9

Relaxation is important so that you can feel good and continue to manifest powerfully. Therefore, you will manifest something that is good for your body. A massage, a day at the spa, a face mask, a foot bath, or something else where you can just sit back and relax. As I said, you don't have to know what's being delivered, just put the frequency of deep relaxation and rest into your energy ball and attract anything that corresponds.

"Hello Universe! Why does my body feel so relaxed? I'm really looking forward to relaxing like this. Thank you!"

What did you experience?

_____

_____

_____

_____

_____

_____

_____

_____

_____

_____

_____

_____

_____

_____

Day 10

You can never have enough friends and even more so good ones! The universe introduces you to a new friend. Maybe at the café, at the supermarket or at work ... Who knows!!!

"Dear Universe, I'm meeting a new friend. I look forward to making this new acquaintance. Thank you so much!"

What did you manifest?

_____

_____

_____

_____

_____

_____

_____

_____

_____

_____

_____

_____

_____

_____

_____

_____

_____

Day 11

Well, any plans yet? How about having someone take you out? Why don't you place your order with the Universe that you will be invited out? An evening at the movies, a restaurant or a bar sounds good, doesn't it? With whom you spend this evening, the universe may decide.

"Good morning universe, I receive an invitation! I'm looking forward to a nice evening. Thank you."

What have you been up to?

_____

_____

_____

_____

_____

_____

_____

_____

_____

_____

_____

_____

_____

_____

_____

_____

_____

Day 12

You've been waiting for a sign or an answer or a hint that will make it easier for you to make a certain decision? The Universe will deliver the answer or clue you need to make your decision.

"Dear Universe! Thank you for giving me the sign that will help me find an answer and make a decision!"

What did you experience?

_____

_____

_____

_____

_____

_____

_____

_____

_____

_____

_____

_____

_____

_____

_____

_____

_____

_____

_____

Day 13

You have your own business? Then now is the time to do something good for your business. You're attracting energy today from something that is beneficial to your business. Maybe it's new clients, an idea for a new marketing strategy, or just a day when everything is running smoothly. I often do this by defining the type of clients I wish to have and then putting them in my energy ball and attracting them. If you are employed and wish for a new job, why not put a new job into your energy ball and attract a new employer.

"Hello Universe, I am happy that my business is going so great! Thank you for all the new clients and projects, dear universe."

What did you manifest?

_____

_____

_____

_____

_____

_____

_____

_____

_____

_____

_____

_____

Day 14

You'll have a great idea. A real flash of inspiration. You will come up with something crazy. And it can be anything really. Maybe it's a brand-new idea that will bring change into your life. However, try not to have any specific expectations and open the gates for magic and miracles to the universe. In your energy ball you can put the frequencies of creativity, ingenuity, joy, passion, genius and curiosity and see what you attract into your life.

"Hello Universe. Why do I have an extremely great idea? I am willing to be and do anything that is needed for it. Thank you so much!"

What have you been experiencing?

_____
_____
_____
_____
_____
_____
_____
_____
_____
_____
_____
_____
_____
_____

Day 15

Today begins the third week of your 21 Day Miracle Challenge. Do you already notice how much faster you are pulling your wishes into your life? Your manifestation muscles are getting stronger and stronger! Why not test your strength by wishing for a romantic experience? I think romance always ends up short in everyday life. Whether you're taken or single, you're sure to have a romantic surprise. What is the frequency of romance? Best you create a little symphony of love, romance, surprise, wonder, appreciation or the feeling of being something special. Are you getting goosebumps yet?

"Hello dear universe, I am happy to get a romantic surprise! I'm ready to give up everything that doesn't allow this in my life. How can things get even better in my love life now? Thank you so much!"

What did you manifest?

_____

_____

_____

_____

_____

_____

_____

_____

_____

_____

_____

Day 16

Something will happen that will really make you laugh. It will be so funny that you will roll over laughing and your stomach will hurt from laughter. By the way, you can additionally fill the energy ball with more of your own wishes every day, it all fits in. The universe knows no limits and neither does your energy ball.

"Dear Universe! Why do I attract a situation into my life that really makes me laugh? I'm going to laugh harder than I have in a long time. I'm already filled with anticipation! Thank you for this fun moment."

What did you experience?

_____
_____
_____
_____
_____
_____
_____
_____
_____
_____
_____
_____
_____
_____
_____
_____

Day 17

Your Miracle Challenge is slowly coming to an end. Your faith in the universe may have long since reached the next level. With this bullish faith, you will manifest health or healing today. Do you often feel tired or can you think of something your body needs support with? Give into the energy ball today the energy of health, healing, love, fitness, strength, vitality and life energy to boost your self-healing powers and have an energetic day. The Universe may also provide impulses for you to eat healthier in the future.

"Hello Universe! I am happy that my body is so healthy and vital and full of life energy! Thank you for drawing all of this into my life with so much ease!"

What did you manifest?

_____
_____
_____
_____
_____
_____
_____
_____
_____
_____
_____
_____

Day 18

It's time again for an extra dose of love, don't you think? That's why you're going to manifest happiness in love. Whether you are already happily engaged or still waiting for your better half, you will experience love. In this exercise, you can also put appreciation, compliments, a confession of love, a loving hug or a passionate kiss into the energy ball. Anything you can think of on the topic of love. Go really deep into the energy of love as you attract the appropriate frequencies. Let's see what else is vibrating on the frequency of love. Anyway, love is on the agenda today!

"Dear Universe, why do I feel so loved? Thank you."

What have you been experiencing?

_____

_____

_____

_____

_____

_____

_____

_____

_____

_____

_____

_____

_____

Day 19

Today, we're really diving into the frequency of gratitude all day, so all your life areas get a little energy boost. You can never be grateful enough. Gratitude is often the key to breaking through blocks. When you are one with the Universe and forming your energy ball, feel the energy of gratitude and pull it in from all sides from the Universe.

"Dear Universe, why do I have so many reasons to be grateful? Thank you that my life is so blessed."

What did you manifest?

_____
_____
_____
_____
_____
_____
_____
_____
_____
_____
_____
_____
_____
_____
_____
_____
_____

Day 20

Expectations are a huge miracle killer, by the way, so it's much easier to attract the energy of wishes and let the universe decide what's best for you. If you want to manifest or attract something specific and that's also a bigger thing for you – where you unconsciously attach expectations to and have the view that that's the only thing you want – then you may end up blocking yourself with that. So, if you're wondering why we're always working with the frequencies in this challenge, hopefully you've noticed by now that it opens your doors to Wonderland a lot more and allows you to invite a lot more wonder into your life as a fixed point of view of something would. Sometimes we go through everyday life quite automatically and therefore often experience the same things and far too few new adventures. So today let's put on a dose of enthusiasm and adventure into the energy ball.

"Dear Universe, thank you for making me go through the day so enthusiastically today! What new adventure am I experiencing? A thousand thanks! Now how can it get any better than this?"

What have you experienced?

_____

_____

_____

_____

_____

_____

_____

Day 21

Today is the last day of your Miracle Challenge. What do you want to manifest next? Today you will freely decide how big a wish you will manifest. Will you dare to manifest a wish today that seemed far away when you started reading this book? With your experience, it should be very easy and quick now. If you don't have an idea, we'll order you a miracle today.

"Dear Universe, I am experiencing a miracle that knocks my socks off, in a positive sense of course! Great, I'm glad and thank you!"

What miracle did you experience?

_____

_____

_____

_____

_____

_____

_____

_____

_____

_____

_____

_____

_____

_____

_____

_____

After the 21 Day Miracle Challenge, I recommend you repeat the exercise on one wish for several days in a row. The more energy, the more miracles! And don't forget, the whole thing should be fun.

On that note, may you be blessed with many miracles!

"There are only two ways to live.
Either as if nothing were a miracle or
as if everything were a miracle."

— Albert Einstein

Reference List

Endnotes

1. Gary Douglas, Dr. Dain Heer. 2010. *Magic. You are it. Be it.* Access Consciousness Publishing Ltd. Santa Barbara, California.
2. Alla Svirinskaya. 2019. *Own your Energy: Develop Immunity to Toxic Energy and Preserve Your Authentic Life Force.* Hay House UK Ltd., London.
3. Deepak Chopra M.D.. 2019. *Metahuman: Unleashing Your Infinite Potential.* Harmony Books, New York.
4. Michael Beckwith. 2013. *Life Visioning: A Transformative Process for Activating Your Unique Gifts and Highest Potential.* Sounds True Inc. Boulder, Colorado.
5. Lynne McTaggert, Gisela Kretzschmar. 2007. *Das Nullpunktfeld: Auf der Suche nach der kosmischen Ur-Energie.* Goldmann Verlag. München.
6. Dr. Joe Dispenza, *Zugang zur Datenbank der unbegrenzten Möglichkeiten.* https://drjoedispenza.de/blog/zugang-zur-datenbank-der-unbegrenzten-moeglichkeiten/ (abgerufen am 15.01.2020).
7. Deepak Chopra, Menas Kafatos. 2018. *Du bist das Universum: Entdecke deine kosmisches Selbst.* Irisiana Verlag. München.
8. Deepak Chopra, Menas Kafatos. 2018. *Du bist das Universum: Entdecke deine kosmisches Selbst.* Irisiana Verlag. München.

9. Deepak Chopra M.D.. 2019. *Metahuman: Unleashing Your Infinite Potential.* Harmony Books. New York.

10. William Walker Atkinson, Drei Eingeweihte. 2011. *Kybalion – Die 7 hermetischen Gesetze: Das Original.* Aurinia Verlag. Hamburg.

11. Anne E. Angelheart. 2007. *Twelve Universal Laws: The Truth That Will Transform Your Life.* Balboa Press. Bloomington, In.

12. Gabby Bernstein. *The #1 Key to Manifesting.* https://gabbybernstein.com/the-1-key-to-manifesting/ (abgerufen am 12.12.2019).

13. Dean Radin, PhD. 2018. *Real Magic: Ancient Wisdom, Modern Science, and a Guide to the Secret Power of the Universe.* Harmony Books. New York.

14. Louise Hay, Mona Lisa Schulz. 2019. *Heile deine Gedanken, heile dein Leben: Innere Balance finden durch Affirmationen und ganzheitliche Medizin.* Heyne Verlag. München.

15. Lynne McTaggart, Isolde Seidel. 2013. *Intention: Mit Gedankenkraft die Welt verändern, Globale Experimente mit fokussierter Energie.* VAK Verlag. Kirchzarten.

16. Lynne McTaggart, Isolde Seidel. 2013. *Intention: Mit Gedankenkraft die Welt verändern, Globale Experimente mit fokussierter Energie.* VAK Verlag. Kirchzarten.

17. Dolores Ashcroft-Nowicki, J.H. Brennan. *Magical Use of Thoughtforms.* Llewellyn, St. Paul, USA.

18. Jose Silva. 1978. *The Silva Mind Control Method.* Pocket Books. New York.

19. Kevin Trudeau.2009. *The hidden Secret of The Law Of Attraction* [GIN]. Audio-CD.The Global Information Network. New York.

20. Dr. Joe Dispenza. 2017. *Werde übernatürlich: Wie gewöhnliche Menschen das Ungewöhnliche erreichen.* Koha-Verlag. Burgrain.

21. Dr. Dain Heer. 2013. *Being you, changing the world*. Access Consciousness Publishing. Santa Barbara, California.

22. Dr. Joe Dispenza. 2017. *Werde übernatürlich: Wie gewöhnliche Menschen das Ungewöhnliche erreichen*. Koha-Verlag. Burgrain.

23. Gary Douglas, Dr. Dain Heer. 2010. *Magic. You are it. Be it.* Access Consciousness Publishing Ltd. Santa Barbara, California.

24. Vishen Lakhiani. 2019. *The Code of the Extraordinary Mind*. Second Edition. Rodale Books. New York.

25. YouAreCreators. *How to Speed Up Manifestations Using This Simple Breathing Technique!* https://www.youtube.com/watch?v=QxEn-12LQ43U (abgerufen am 13.12.2019).

26. Dr. Dain Heer. 2011. *Sei du selbst und verändere die Welt*. Scorpio Verlag. München.

27. Jose Silva. 1978. *The Silva Mind Control Method*. Pocket Books. New York.

28. Neville Goddard. 2010. *Feeling is the Secret*. Pacific Publishing Studio.

29. Cuddy, Amy J.C., Caroline A. Wilmuth, and Dana R. Carney. 2012. *The Benefit of Power Posing Before a High-Stakes Social Evaluation*. Harvard Business School Working Paper, No. 13-027.

30. Michael Beckwith. *How to bring on the Vibration of Strength*. https://www.youtube.com/watch?v=_F4Mvwc0gvU (abgerufen am 3.2.2020).

31. Michael Beckwith. 201. *Life Visioning: A Transformative Process for Activating Your Unique Gifts and Highest Potential*. Sounds True Publishing. Boulder, Colorado.

32. Louise Hay. 2016. *Finde deine Lebenskraft: Wie Affirmationen unser Leben verändern*. Ullstein Taschenbuch. Berlin.

33. David R. Hawkins. 2014. *Die Ebenen des Bewusstseins: Von der Kraft die wir ausstrahlen.* VAK Verlags GmbH. Kirchzarten.

34. Gay Hendricks. 2010. *The Big Leap: Conquer Your Hidden Fear and Take Life to the Next Level.* Harper Collings. New York.

35. Gabrielle Bernstein. 2019. *Super Attractor. Methods for manifesting a life beyond your wildest dreams.* Hay House, Inc.. New York.

36. Debrah Landwehr Engle. 2014. *Sieben kleine Worte: Das einzige Gebet, was Sie wirklich brauchen können.* Heyne. München.

37. Michael Singer. 2016. *Die Seele will frei sein: Eine Reise zu sich selbst.* Ullstein Verlag.Berlin.

38. Michael Singer. 2007. *The Untethered Soul: The Journey Beyond Yourself.* New Harbinger Publications. Oakland, California.

39. Michael Singer, Onlinekurs „Living from a place of surrender". https://www.soundstrue.com/store/living-from-a-place-of-surrender?sq=1#a_aid=5dfbb27a13fea&a_bid=7acfaed4 (abgerufen am 03.02.2020).

40. Michael Singer, Onlinekurs „Living from a place of surrender". https://www.soundstrue.com/store/living-from-a-place-of-surrender?sq=1#a_aid=5dfbb27a13fea&a_bid=7acfaed4 (abgerufen am 03.02.2020).

41. Dr. Sue Morter. 2019. *The Energy Codes: The 7-Step System to Awaken Your Spirit, Heal Your Body, and Live Your Best Life.* Atria Books. New York.

42. Dr. Bradley Nelson. 2019. *The Emotion Code: How to Release Your Trapped Emotions for Abundant Health, Love and Happiness.* First St. Martins Edition. New York.

43. Dr. Wayne W. Dyer. 2015. *I can see clearly now.* Hay House, USA.

44. Adrian Cho. 2017. *Quantum experiment in space confirms that reality is what you make it.* https://www.sciencemag.org/news/2017/10/quantum-experiment-space-confirms-reality-what-you-make-it-0 (abgerufen am 05.02.2020).

45. Vianna Stibal. 2012. *ThetaHealing für Fortgeschrittene*. Ullstein Taschenbuch Verlag. Berlin.

46. Vianna Stibal. 2012. *ThetaHealing für Fortgeschrittene*. Ullstein Taschenbuch Verlag. Berlin.

47. Tad James, Wyatt Woodsmall. 1994. *Timeline – NLP Konzepte*. Junfermann Verlag. Paderborn.

48. Reagan Hillyer. *This is how you can manifest your ideal reality*. https://www.youtube.com/watch?v=6pNG9GLDzZM (abgerufen am 07.02.2020).

About the author

The author runs a company with 4-6 freelancers. For the past years she has been passionately devoting her free time to the subject of manifestation and energy healing. With this book she wants to inspire people to believe in miracles and magic again.

Printed in Great Britain
by Amazon

27304071R00088